How to Work with a Virtual Assistant - Outsource Everything but Your Brilliance

Kathy Soulsby

Contents

Introduction

Welcome, and thank you for choosing this book. I see you! You do not have enough hours in the day.

Maybe you're barely keeping your head above water getting the work done for your business. Bits are creeping into evenings and weekends, and your family, friends, and energy levels are starting to complain. You absolutely know that your business could run less chaotically if you only had an extra pair of hands.

Maybe you have a looming sense of dread, convinced there are lurking areas of the business that will one day—not today, not tomorrow, but one day—cause you terrible stress because you simply don't have the time now to look at them properly. You're sticking a plaster on an open wound and hoping it won't bleed out before you have the time to do a proper job with some stitches. But that spare time to sit down and look at the issue properly just hasn't materialised.

Maybe you work in a bigger business, but you don't see daylight outside of meetings. You have no time to do any actual work because your time is booked back-to-back, and you haven't found a way to unravel that.

Or maybe your business is poised to grow. It's an exciting time, but with growth comes extra work that you aren't sure you have the bandwidth for.

You need help, you need time, and you need a solution.

So, you're wondering: Could a Virtual Assistant be the right solution for you and your business?

In a nutshell, a Virtual Assistant, or VA, is a freelance resource that supports multiple companies. Their skills vary, but most are extremely organised and flexible and will help you with such tasks as inbox management, diary management, client booking, researching, invoicing and general administration. They typically bill by time, so you only pay for hours used. They only work for you for a certain amount of time in any given week or month.

A good VA can work alongside you and take your business from frantic to thriving. No small claim, I know, but I've seen it happen over and over again. They can give you time back to do the vital things in your business that you and only you can do. They'll skim off your task list everything that you don't need to be involved with and probably even help you create and manage that task list so that everyone knows what they are doing and when. As well as doing tasks, the right VA can work alongside you and learn your business, helping you to meet your goals and suggesting ways to make things run more smoothly.

A VA can free up your time and energy, allowing you to focus on the work in the business that you are critical for. You can get off the hamster wheel of constant doing and have more space and time to think.

And you might well find that you can balance work and life better once you have another pair of hands helping.

Expense receipts won't be a Saturday morning chore when you can send them on for your VA to do.

I realise that hiring your first assistant may feel like a big step, particularly if it's the first long-term hire that your business has made. But it doesn't need to be nerve-wracking. Although it may feel terrifying, I'm going to talk you through it, step by step. After reading this book you'll have all the knowledge and the tools you need to find, hire and keep an amazing VA.

If you've tried working with a VA before and it didn't work out, but you aren't sure why, then I hope the information in this book will give you some insight, help you find someone that's a better fit for you and your business, and make your next experience with a VA a more positive one.

Positive VA experiences are, after all, at the heart of my own business. I've been a VA myself since 2014 and have since grown my business to an agency, Personally Virtual, of over 30 VAs. Our clients are a mixture of one-man or one-woman businesses, small businesses, and multi-national firms turning over millions. Household names and many more you will never have heard of.

Over the last decade, I've had countless conversations with prospective clients, work friends and connections, many of whom just don't know where to start with "this VA thing". Perhaps someone has suggested it to them because they are drowning in work, or they've heard it might be a thing but really don't understand how it works or where to start. Some people have picked up a business book and come across the term VA in an international context and wonder if that is how UK VAs work (spoiler alert, it probably isn't). Some have seen friends and colleagues with a fabulous VA and think it might be a good solution for them.

Through many hundreds of conversations with clients and prospects, certain questions about VAs and working with them have come up again and again. I got tired of repeating myself! No, not really. But I did feel it was time to collect the answers to those common questions in one place for easy access. And as the VA industry has grown and more freelancers use the term "Virtual Assistant," it's become more complicated—and ever more important to a successful VA experience—to work out what these VAs do and don't do.

With a great VA / client relationship, it's a strategic partnership. A good VA will be learning about you, your business and the future goals that have been set, whether that's for you as an individual or for the company as a whole or both. You work together to achieve the aims of the business. If your VA knows what the goal is, they can help you manage the day-to-day work to get there and ensure that your time is targeted where it needs to be.

There are surprisingly few books written about the Executive Assistant (or Virtual Assistant, in this case) working partnership from the point of view of the client or boss, the onus seems to be very much on the EA or VA to manage upwards. For you, putting some effort into this can make the most phenomenal difference to your business, your working life and (getting) a life outside of work. Whether you are founder / owner of a start-up or a leader in a larger firm, having a superb assistant can make a huge impact.

Being brutally honest, it was time to write this book in 2018, but I just couldn't do it. My previous book, Virtually Painless, was published in 2017. After it came out, I couldn't write so much as a shopping list for a year. I was all written out. And then life got busy. Really busy. And then we had a pandemic where lots of people had time to redecorate, but VAs just seemed to work even harder, me included.

So, what happened? Why now?

I got myself another VA.

I've had one for years, the amazing Laura, but I finally realised there was more I could and should delegate and that my brain was full. Full to the brim. I had the conversation with myself that I've had with many clients and decided I needed more resource in my own business. A conversation with Laura revealed that she didn't have capacity to take on more hours, so I searched for someone else to add.

Less than a month after finding my second VA, Helen, I had the headspace and time to finally crack on with something I should have done five years ago. That's the power of a good VA right there! Between them, Laura and Helen cover many of the day-to-day things that were cluttering up my time and my brain. They are also both amazing cheerleaders, accountability partners, and moral support. Don't underestimate the power of that when you are embarking on a big project that feels like it may never end.

Hiring and working with these two wonderful VAs— and walking many clients through it—has given me the client perspective on the process. But in my time in the VA industry, I've worked with VA-client relationships from every angle. I have matched hundreds of VAs with clients. I've trawled LinkedIn, Facebook and online sites for great associates (and rejected a lot of the not-so-great ones). I've seen VA-client relationships flourish and flounder.

In the writing of this book, I have also interviewed and surveyed both VAs and their clients to get their views on what makes a great partnership and what drives them crazy. It was a joy to listen to them describe fantastic relationships where VAs have directly impacted on the clients' business. But, as you might expect, there are some horror stories out there of vanishing VAs, bad payers, poor behaviour and lunatic expectations. I think there are war stories in every industry — where there are people, there are unhappy and unpleasant people, and they are best avoided. But don't worry. This book contains plenty of red flags and pointers that will help you avoid becoming part of a horror story yourself.

You'll find concrete action steps highlighted at the end of every chapter. Complete them to create a foundation for the information in each subsequent chapter. Or complete them when you're ready to hire a VA, to be fully ready to hit the ground running.

One aspect of working with a VA that makes many of us want to run in the opposite direction is the legal and data protection side of things. I'm one of those only-deal-with-it-because-I-have-to folks, so I've brought in expert Annabel Kaye to assuage our fears and help us understand the details. Annabel runs KoffeeKlatch, a legal firm set up specifically to work with freelancers, in particular VAs. She has deep knowledge about IR35 (the off-payroll working regulations in the UK), GDPR (The

General Data Protection Regulations) and all manner of other key information that is relevant to a VA-client relationship. She also has about nine VAs on her own team! In a whole bonus chapter at the end of the book, Annabel gives you essential information on keeping your business safe while working with a VA and other legal aspects of outsourcing in the UK. (Flip to the back of the book if you're really excited about it!)

But before we get there, we'll start with the foundational part of the VA-client relationship that you know best: you, and what you need.

You'll learn how to think about your current role and the kinds of work that you do by differentiating your unique brilliance from the tasks that are just your job (or rightfully someone else's). We'll look at why it's crucial to make time and space to do the things you are brilliant at, then start thinking about what tasks you can sensibly outsource to someone else. We'll then do some sense-checking of you and your business as they are now to find out whether this is the right time to be bringing in support.

Assuming that it is, we'll then get in depth and look at the types of assistants that are out there to get you thinking about how your support might look, what your non-negotiables are, and whether there are any particular skills or experiences that you want to be sure to look for when you get into hiring.

I'll then give you some insight into the world of Virtual Assistants so that when you're talking with them you have a clear understanding of how it works and what a VA can really do for you when you have the right one. We'll also look at ways to make that relationship between you the best it can be.

I deliberately leave the hiring section until quite near the end. By the time we reach this point in the book you'll have a really clear idea of what and who you should be looking for as you begin the process of finding your new VA. You'll understand the logistics and the options so you can approach the hiring conversation with confidence. And I'll give you some handy examples and questions for you to customise to your own needs so you can be sure to find a VA that is both professionally set up and right for you.

In the later chapters we'll make sure that you are well prepared to onboard your VA as efficiently and thoroughly as possible. And we'll think about day to day working strategies to build in so that you get off on the right foot.

And lastly, we go through FAQs and fears to address any niggling concerns and some troubleshooting tips you can use if things aren't going quite to plan.

With the information in these pages, you'll be able to determine if help from a Virtual Assistant is what you need right now. If it is, you'll know what to expect, how to find and hire the right VA for you, and how to ensure a great partnership that will help you grow your business and free you up to do what you do best.

Ready to begin? Let's start with your brilliance.

One

Outsource Everything but Your Brilliance

The main reason to use an assistant is to free up your time so you can do what you are brilliant at.

What is your brilliance?

Can you go into an organisation and help them fix their culture? Can you coach people to stand up in front of a crowd of people and hold them spellbound for 30 minutes? Can you help people advertise their business to new clients? Are you a writer? A teacher? A plumber? A philosopher or a biochemist?

Everyone has that thing, that spark, that talent they do brilliantly. What's yours? What is the thing that you sell, essentially, in the case of most service businesses? Or is your brilliance the selling, having those meetings with prospects and getting new business into the organisation?

Understanding your brilliance is key to thinking about outsourcing. Your brilliance is what needs to be protected. It's not simply what you **can** do, but what you must do. We can all do many things, but there's a strong chance others can do them as well. What we're looking for here is the bit that is just you. If you're not sure what it is, think about what you're doing when you are most in a flow state—that's usually a sign that you are in your zone of genius. Time flies, it doesn't feel like work, and it is deeply satisfying, even if it is also sometimes challenging.

We all have things we are amazing at. And things that we're less amazing at. Finding a role that only consists of the first set of things is nigh on impossible, even in a business that you set up yourself. Every role has a certain amount of "stuff" that surrounds it. Somewhat ironically, often the better you are at your brilliance, the quicker you get promoted or the more clients you get and then the less of your brilliance you get to do on a daily basis. Success seems to breed administrative tasks!

Let's say you are a novelist. Your brilliance is writing fantastic crime thrillers that people love to read. The writing element is your brilliance: creating plots and characterisation and managing the pace of the action.

If you want your work to be read, then the books must be published, which is going to involve all manner of pitches, meetings, reviews, edits, decisions around covers and more. Then you'll market the book, so people know that it is out there. We're probably talking launch events, endless PR emails to drum up local or national press coverage, maybe some tours of bookshops and a lot of social media. These things will all need booking into your diary and coordinating, especially if it's a tour. You might need a website, social media feeds to pump with promotional posts, and marketing bumph to send out to booksellers. You might need to navigate Kindle versions and audio books of your creations as well. Once the money starts coming in, you'll need to manage your finances, track expense receipts and mileage from those bookshop trips and pay some taxes. If your book is a hit, then you may have fan letters (or emails and DMs) to manage. It's a long list. And while you are busy doing this list, you aren't doing the thing that is your brilliance.

Maybe you are a director in a small consultancy. You were employed because you are amazing with people, drawing out the nuances of complex businesses and human needs. You have a quick mind and can think in ways others can't to solve problems. You have a Finance department, so you don't do much in the way of billing, there's a Marketing department and PR agency and none of that really falls under your remit anyway. But are you the one getting workshops and meetings booked? Organising post-it notes, Miro boards, and catering? Researching flights and trains? For your internal commitments are you having to go back and forth on meeting slots? Do you have a guilty pile of your own expense receipts even as you send out notes to the team telling them to process expenses promptly at the end of the month? Are you holding a lot of mental load around the next follow ups with prospects or things that need to go into the diary later in the year?

As you can see, even in a company that has back-office support, a busy role can have things that need doing — well outside of your brilliance.

The costs of doing it all

It would be easy enough to say "Well, I can do everything, so I might as well. I can just about fit it in". That may be the case, but your brilliance is the key here. How much does your brilliance cost? How much do you sell it for? And how much energy do you need to conserve in order to preserve it?

First let's look at the financial aspect. Some industries are much more focused on selling billable time than others. Lawyers, for example, know exactly what their brilliance is worth, and most will have a target number of hours to bill. Plumbers know their hourly rate, as do coaches and therapists. Most consultants have a day rate.

What does your brilliance sell for? And do you want to have more of it to sell? You'll almost certainly pay an assistant less per hour than you charge for your brilliance. So financially, working with an assistant who can give you even thirty minutes a day back to sell is a no brainer.

You're a freelance consultant. You bill out to clients at £4,000 a day. If you're spending about four hours a week doing your business administration, you're potentially losing £2000 a week. Or you could be making the best use of that downtime by posting on LinkedIn or networking to line up future projects. Or you could be getting to the gym three times a week and going to watch your daughter play football and giving your brain some space to be a genius. That is what four hours gives—or costs—you.

If you hired a VA for those four hours a week, it might cost you £150-200 but it gives you back your time, at your rate, to do what you need to do. Or you get to have a little downtime and rest between sessions so that each client absolutely gets the best version of you when they meet you.

Or you're a coach. You bill clients £1000 for every one-hour session. Your brilliance is your coaching style and the results you get. There is a limit to how many of those you can deliver a week, not least because you need prep time for sessions, time to write them up, and time to rest and regroup afterwards. You can't just bash out seven sessions in a day back-to-back (if you can, you are hard core and I take my hat off to you).

After all, time and cost aren't the only factors that need to be considered when you are talking about protecting your brilliance. Energy and distraction are "costs" as well. Costs to your business and absolutely a cost to your energy levels and efficiency.

If you aren't billing fulltime, say you bill six hours of client work a week, there is an argument to say that you can, in your non-billing time, manage all the surrounding admin. And that may be the case.

I'd question though whether that is the best use of your time and energy when you could be using it to find better clients or resting your amazing brain to give your brilliance some time to shine. As one of my clients said recently, "If you've only got 100 units of energy a day are you going to spend 50 of those doing email?"

It's really tempting when things are busy to just throw more time at the problem. To work more hours and to let work slide into the evening just to get ahead a little before the next day. We've all glanced at our phones to see if there aren't any quick emails we can bash out while catching up on a bit of Netflix. But ending a workday properly and completely is important to our brains.

Cal Newport, who literally wrote the book on deep work, says of using evenings to catch up: "If you keep interrupting your evening to check and respond to e-mail or put aside a few hours after dinner to catch up on an approaching deadline, you're robbing your directed attention centers of the uninterrupted rest they need for restoration." He explains "Even if these work dashes consume only a small amount of time, they prevent you from reaching the levels of deeper relaxation in which attention restoration can occur. Only the confidence that you're done with work until the next day can convince your brain to downshift to the level where it can begin to recharge for the next day to follow."

Or as he sums it up, "Trying to squeeze a little more work out of your evenings might reduce your effectiveness the next day enough that you end up getting less done than if you had instead respected a shutdown."[1]

Rest and recuperation are vital in protecting and maintaining your brilliance, not to mention your sanity. And "rest" can include having a break from a head full of tasks and things that need to be done. A busy headspace is not an easy place to relax in.

In his book "When: The Scientific Secrets of Perfect Timing", Daniel Pink looks at the impact of taking breaks on performance. "Restorative breaks enhance performance. Lunches and naps help us elude the trough and get more and better work done in the

---

[1] Cal Newport, Deep Work: Rules for Focused Success in a Distracted World

afternoon. A growing body of science makes it clear: Breaks are not a sign of sloth but a sign of strength."[2]

We humans just aren't geared up to work hell-for-leather for eight hours straight (or longer), and when we do, mistakes happen. We can't reach our full potential. If your solution to the problem is to work harder and longer, you may not be anywhere near as effective as you think.

It's also clear to me, for myself and for many clients I have seen, that brilliance often isn't the kind of thing you can shove into thirty-minute slots. Often, brilliance needs space. Space for deep work, thinking, and energy to do those things. If your brain is cluttered with a hundred other things that need doing, it's unlikely that you'll be able to sit down and say "right, brilliance time. I've got 40 minutes to have an amazing idea for this project, let's go!" It just doesn't work like that. Apart from the brain space, you also need the brain ease and time to just be. Not rushing from task to task and meeting to meeting like a ball in a pinball machine.

---

[2] Daniel Pink, When: The Scientific Secrets of Perfect Timing

Many people I have spoken to say they get their best ideas or solutions to problems when they are walking the dog, or at the gym, or just out for a coffee with a friend. Our busy brains are remarkable, but having space to do other things is key to keeping them that way.

Another thing that I find interesting is that people think it's more efficient if they can do everything in their business, without considering whether they are skilled at them or not! I remember having a conversation with one business owner who taught himself how to build websites so he could create his own website. How long did that take? And then was it any good? And did he teach himself enough to know about regular updates and patches or changes in the law which might mean a year on from the build some new things should be added? That can't have been a good use of his time unless he genuinely had nothing else to do in his business.

I'm all for learning new skills and I do think it's helpful to have a bit of understanding of everything that happens in your own business. But spending all the time and effort to learn a new skill of that magnitude just to do it once, seems a bit crazy to me. We're going to look at this in a little more detail in Chapter Seven because whilst I wouldn't recommend you train as a VA before you get one, you absolutely should always have the knowledge about how the processes in your business run if you needed to—if your VA were to be abducted by aliens, or ill or whatever. So, you need some failsafe processes in place so that you, or someone else in the business are never in a position that you don't know how your own business works. But that doesn't mean that you need to go and learn how to code!

Delete, automate, delegate

By now, I hope I've convinced you that your brilliance is worth protecting, for your sake and the sake of your business. Now it's time to get really clear on how you spend your time—what tasks are your brilliance, what tasks are not, but need you to get them done anyway, and what tasks you should not be doing at all. It's the first step in deciding whether you need to outsource some work.

First things first: write a big, long list of everything that you do. Get detailed. Keep adding to it as we go along, because you almost certainly do more than you realise.

If it helps, think back to a recent, fairly standard day, start at the beginning and work through. You can even think outside of work if you need to because you may start your day thinking about having to look up travel times to get to where you need to be that day. The more specific you can be, the better. And list everything from the trivial right up to the key work of the day.

Deleting

Some things you spend your time doing may be totally pointless. I know that feels like a strange thing to say, but how many meetings do you go to and how many are really relevant for you? Are there any that you can remove from your diary? Or send a delegate to instead?

Are you being too generous with your time? I once created a flow chart for an old boss about whether or not to say yes to a meeting or event.

The last option was "would you rather be watching Top Gear with a glass of red at home?" He was one of life's radiators and was very generous with his time. But he needed to delete some meetings from his schedule so that both he and his business could function at their best.

It's nice to be nice. I have many conversations with those thinking about getting a VA and those who want to become a VA. With most of these calls, I know in advance the person will not be right for either my team (if they want to be a VA) or my client base (if they are looking for a VA). But I'll have the calls anyway to help them out. However, I have a set number I'll do a week and they must work for my diary. I'm all for paying it forward but not at the expense of things that are vital to my business. Consider where, if anywhere, setting some boundaries like this might help you.

There is a large amount of admin that goes into any role. Some of it is necessary to make the wheels of life go around. But there are probably some things that you can cheerfully chuck out of your life. Reports you create that are never read, updates that are too frequent, reworking of things that already exist elsewhere. As you look at your task list with fresh eyes, are there things you do that are…ahem…a bit overkill?

As an example, one client I worked with used to religiously file his emails into folders by client and project. He received hundreds of emails a day and this filing process was taking him twenty minutes a day. That's more than an hour a week lost that he could have spent on something more financially remunerative or personally fulfilling—all "just in case" he ever needed to find something, and the search function couldn't manage it.

Look, I file my emails, too. You better believe that my inbox is a thing of zen beauty. Of course it is, I'm a VA and I am obsessed with productivity! So, I file, but I file in big chunks, because realistically, the time I save **not** filing into hundreds of folders is much greater than the time I'd spend once every year when I need to track down a specific email and it takes me five minutes instead of 30 seconds. I don't think it's worth paying a VA to file emails either, to be honest. Not a backlog anyway. Certainly, having someone keep on top of your inbox is a great move. But filing 40,000 emails going back to 2016? Hell no, life is too short. Move the whole lot into an archive folder and start fresh.

Challenge yourself when it comes to deleting tasks from your list.

Automating

There are entire books on how to automate your business and whole systems to help you do so. How helpful they are to your business very much depends on the type of service or product you deliver. Clearly an online product with little human intervention can be more easily automated than a business that provides a complex service project with lots of human effort involved.

But no matter your kind of business, it's worth thinking about automation wherever you have a task that frequently repeats in a similar way. Look for systemisations that could be brought in to reduce manual input and minimise human effort in useful ways. And a good VA should certainly be able to suggest and quite likely implement some ways of reducing workload, even if that is just creating templates for emails used most frequently or an FAQ document for client queries.

Online booking tools are fantastic for some businesses. MS Bookings, Acuity Scheduling or Calendly will help people find a time in your diary without the back and forth of emails or calls. This is amazing for people with diaries that aren't that busy. It also relies on the user being very diligent about keeping their diary accurate and being very clear on free and busy times. Otherwise, it can easily go horribly wrong, and let's be honest, it isn't everyone's zone of genius. I absolutely wouldn't use these systems for very busy complex diaries—for that, you need a super-smart human brain that can think through solutions and options. A diary ninja, as we call the folks on our team!

You can also use automated diary managers for only parts of your schedule, maybe a specific project or part of a project. As an example, we set Calendly up for one of our clients purely for sets of coaching calls ahead of a workshop. He allocates specific chunks of time, and his VA sets up the tech and asks all the candidates to book in. The VA manages the process so there won't be any "accidents." The result is a much-reduced amount of back and forth on dates for all parties.

Automating certain emails can also save you (or your future assistant) a tremendous amount of time. There are CRMs (Customer Relationship Management Systems) or project systems that can do in-depth automations, but both Outlook and Gmail have a number of addons and built-in functionality to help. They let you automatically bring emails back on a certain date or if no one replies, for example. You can schedule emails to send in the future, letting you batch tasks like sending out pre-work for a workshop or confirmations for events.

You can create template emails for the most common answers to questions. Tools like Quick Steps and Boomerang speed up processes. You can now even run polls in Outlook to take date preferences from people and get a quick consensus on a meeting time (outside of Outlook you can use a Doodle Poll).

Templates and shortcuts, often customisable and useable across any number of systems, reduce the amount of work you have to do from scratch every time. MS forms, Google forms and Typeform make data gathering easy, both for you and the person being asked for the information. Most accountancy packages have an option to automatically send chasing emails for unpaid invoices.

Take a careful look at your tech to find the automatisation gems embedded in your current systems. If that prospect makes your eyes go wild, add the job to the list of things you'll ask your new assistant to take on. A good VA will have suggestions on automation you can use to make things run more smoothly and with minimal effort and cost. (Though for more complex system support, you may well want to hire a specialist VA or tech expert in the systems you use.) There may be some time investment setting things up, but then you should find that you get some glorious time back to put to better use.

Delegating

Finally, if you can't delete it or automate it, you can delegate it. And delegating *well*—so it supports your brilliance and helps your business thrive—is what the remainder of this book is all about.

When you think about tasks to delegate, it can be helpful to split them into several groups. There are the things you don't like doing. Generally, the tasks we don't enjoy tend to fall to the bottom of our lists, so handing these over will make a real impact on your productivity. I don't enjoy doing contracts or form filling, so Helen takes care of that with my input.

Then there are the tasks that you can't do. I am not a visual person, so I always delegate out anything to do with design or graphics; I'd spend way too much time on them and even then, they'd be awful!

Finally, there are the things you shouldn't do – even if you quite enjoy them. Be honest about whether it is appropriate and sensible for you to be doing certain tasks in the context of your overall role. Just because you can do something and you don't hate it, doesn't mean you should do it! I take a strange satisfaction from reconciling my accounts in Xero, but it isn't the best use of my time, that's Laura's zone of genius and if I find myself meddling in it, I will make myself stop!

Note that, while VAs are perfect folks to delegate to, one size does not fit all. Depending on the type of task you are delegating and its complexity, you may need more than one VA, with different skillsets. Or if it's a project like a rebrand or a new website, your VA may manage it with another supplier, getting your input as and when needed. We'll go into detail on how to find the right VA or VAs for you in Chapter Six.

A VA may be able to help you with tasks like these:

TASK LIST

- Inbox management (your emails)
- Customer service-type emails
- Calendar management
- Appointment booking
- Travel booking
- Blog writing
- Social media posts
- Managing expense receipts
- Sending invoices
- Chasing up late payers
- Creating PowerPoint decks
- Typing (audio typing and copy typing)
- Pulling together actions and managing task lists
- Updating CRMs
- Data entry
- Ordering books, gifts and cards
- Document creation, e.g., contracts or purchase orders
- Research
- Creating online forms and surveys
- Recruitment support
- Tracking prospects
- Proofreading
- Minute taking
- Podcast editing
- Website building
- PR
- Copywriting

Example Task List

As well as specific tasks, I think it's helpful to look at categories, or levels, of tasks. In "The Replaceable

Founder", Ari Meisel talks about the six levels of delegation. Meisel's framework may help you think through which tasks you want to delegate now and which you might want to in the future. The levels of delegation will certainly impact on your choice of VA if you choose to hire one. They're listed here in order of increasing responsibility:

1. Simple tasks, like buying a book online.
2. More complex tasks that involve some research, like booking a flight.
3. Research with additional advice, like selecting a shortlist of suppliers and making suggestions as to which is the best option.
4. Some outward-facing responsibility: you might get them to engage that new supplier and liaise with them to complete a project, just giving you updates.
5. Decisioning-making authority: within some parameters your delegate has the power to make autonomous decisions.

6. Full authority to handle a complex area of the business.[3]

Generally, your VA will be working between level one and four. Some trusted assistants might eventually get to level five over the course of time. My view is that you'd be unlikely to give a level six level of authority to a freelancer. If you only want a VA working at level 1 you obviously won't need as experienced a person as if you want to build up to delegating at level 4. At the higher levels you'll need someone who really understands your business as they are making decisions on your behalf.

---

[3] Ari Meisel, The Replaceable Founder

A quick pause for a reality check

At this point you might be skipping about with excitement at your new life with a VA and how much easier life will be. Great! Hold that thought. It will be.

However, Nirvana will not be reached overnight.

There is going to be a period of time where everything is harder and takes longer than before and you will question whether this is worth the effort.

This is totally normal.

When you are used to doing everything yourself, having to show someone else how to do it, how you want it, and when, feels painful. Because it is. The urge to just say "never mind, I'll do it this time, it'll be quicker" will be fighting its way through your brain several times a day. Don't give in! Just accept that in the first few weeks of onboarding someone and getting them up to speed, it will take longer to get work done and you may find yourself working more. This is to be expected. There are certainly things you can do to make onboarding quicker and more seamless (see Chapter Seven for some specific support on this) but they still involve you investing time in them.

There will be a bunch of "quick win" simple tasks you can hand over at once. Enjoy them. But the more complex tasks, getting into the real webbing of your world, take longer. And you don't want to make the mistake of dumping everything on your new VA immediately. So please be patient or you will overwhelm them.

Now that I've brought you back down to reality with a gentle bump, we're going to stay here. It's time to check whether outsourcing is right for you—and right for you right now.

***

ACTION STEPS

1. Create a detailed, comprehensive list of everything you do each day, week, and month.
2. Separate the list into three groups based on how you define your brilliance:
    a. Tasks to delete (be realistic and ruthless!).
    b. Tasks to automate.
    c. Tasks to delegate (includes tasks you don't like, tasks you don't or can't do well, and tasks you shouldn't do, even if you like them).

Two

When is the Right Time to Outsource?

Bring in an assistant too early and you don't have enough work for them to do or the budget to do it. Too late and you're potentially already at a volume of work yourself that is excessive, and therefore finding the time to manage recruiting and onboarding a new team member is tricky.

So how do you know when it's the right moment to bring someone into your business as a support? Find out if now is the right time for you by working your way through the questions and quiz in this chapter.

Are you ready to let go?

It might be that a VA is your first experience of someone other than you working in and on your business. You may have IT support or a web designer but a VA, particularly the kind of ongoing support we're talking about in this book, is a little closer to home.

You have to be willing and emotionally ready to delegate some tasks. If absolutely everything up to this point has been done by you, this is going to feel weird. Sometimes nice-weird ("Oh thank God, that's off my list and getting done without me, I hated it") and sometimes annoying, frustrating, or even unhappy-weird ("Why is she doing it that way, that's not how I'd do it!"). But either way, it will feel weird. There are a few ways to balance out the initial weirdness.

Firstly, be cautious and put security and legal measures in place so you know your business is safe (turn to Chapter Six on what to hire for as well as the Bonus Chapter at the back of the book to help with this). Secondly, only delegate to someone you trust. You should only give tasks to someone who understands and respects your business and your values. It is completely fine to only ask your VA to do a few easy internal tasks as they start, to ensure that you're happy with everything before they're let loose on client facing work. But in the fullness of time, you'll need to let your VA take the initiative and make some decisions without your input. Otherwise, they'll be asking you everything at every stage and it'll take longer than if you did it yourself. If you can't imagine a time when you would let that happen, if you know that you tend to micromanage, then be realistic about that now.

It doesn't necessarily mean that a VA won't work—you may just need to manage their expectations at the start and review exactly what you give them in order for you to feel comfortable. Some tasks naturally lend themselves to delegation by those who are more nervous about handing things over. A VA writing your blogs or web content for example, is likely to expect you to review it before it goes live.

However, it's impractical to check every expense receipt that a VA has entered onto your accounting system; if you felt the need to do that it would be ringing alarms bells for me. Likewise, if a VA is managing your diary, you should be able to let them do that without checking each and every appointment change. If this makes you nervous and you feel that you must be involved in every transaction and every email, then you may not be ready for a VA. And of course, it's not going to be very cost effective for you if you routinely check every single task they do.

Do you have enough work to outsource?

You may be ready, willing and poised to get someone onboard but if you don't have enough work that someone else can pick up, you might not get a useful bang for your buck. When we are overwhelmed, it is very easy to think that we have piles and piles of things that someone else could take off us. But is this really the case? Take a careful look at your "delegate" list. As we talked about earlier, there is an initial investment of time and energy to getting a VA on board, and if you only have a teensy bit of work for them to do, it might not be worth it.

If you only send your VA 20 minutes of ad hoc work three times a month, they won't have the opportunity to know your business or add value if they're doing nothing more than one task and then clocking off. Plus, the work won't be at all worthwhile for them. VAs are generally very good at mentally switching between clients. But if it's a week between tasks, and the tasks are bitty at that, it takes more time to remind ourselves what it was we were doing, who's who and what's where. It's kind of a faff. Chances are, as a small client you will end up at the bottom of our priority list.

If you only need eight hours of support a month now (really the bare minimum) but you can clearly see how it will grow, then it is worth getting a great VA in place now, knowing that in the future the role will expand. You and your VA will soon work out once you get started what the volume of work is – whether it is about what you thought, more or less - and you can flex accordingly.

If this is your circumstance, try to create a backup list of tasks for when your VA is short of work from you – or even some ongoing things they can do if you are getting to the end of the month, and you still have hours "in the pot".

Do you have the budget?

Can you pay for enough of a VA's time to make the relationship worthwhile for you—and them?

If you want to build a good relationship with a VA and really have someone be a useful support to you, you need to be able to invest in at least 8-10 hours a month of their time (or get to that amount quickly). To be a valuable business asset, a VA needs to get to understand you and your business and, as mentioned above, that's very hard to do on anything less than those hours. Any less than this is just using your VA as a bit of a task monkey. And that may be ok for now but it's more work for you as you'll have to give instructions every single time. What a waste of a great resource who is more than capable of doing more.

With a decent amount of monthly hours though, you can invest in training your VA. They'll know how you like to work and what your priorities are. They'll be armed to make decisions on your behalf. They'll add value to your business and start to free up your time to earn more money. So, can you pay for that?

The opposite end of this spectrum (and we've all had clients like this, irrespective of industry) is having a list of 40 things that all need doing and a monthly budget of £100. It just isn't going to happen! I recall a prospect I once spoke to who had a shopping list of VA tasks as long as my arm – monthly newsletters to draft and send, quarterly events to organise, fortnightly online masterclasses to support, monthly invoicing and expense receipts as well as complex diary and travel management. Her budget paid for 10 hours a month. It just isn't feasible. A VA is not a miracle worker! I do think because we work "on the clock" we are more efficient than other support workers, but we can't bend time. And just because we are capable of doing multiple things doesn't mean we can fit them all in at once. You aren't going to replace a fulltime PA with a VA doing ten hours a month. It's just not realistic.

All that said, if you know you want a VA but only have a small budget, you'll likely be better off paying for less time from an experienced assistant who will be efficient and fast than for more time from a new, possibly cheaper VA who doesn't have the knowledge or skills to know how to get things done quickly. It's that old adage that you can only pick two of cheap, good or fast. And you probably want the latter two.

Are you trying to fix a person with a resource?

Are you bringing in a VA to fix a problem you have failed to solve with something else? If you are thinking of getting a VA to support someone on the team, is that because they are overloaded or because they are unmanageable?

If you can't manage your member of staff, please don't expect a VA to do it for you. It seems somewhat ludicrous to me, but I have seen it in action. If an employee or manager is a loose cannon, booking flights last minute, costing the business a fortune and constantly changing priorities, not turning up for meetings etc, that's a "them" problem (or a "you" problem) to solve. A VA doesn't have the authority to tell their clients what to do! If the Senior Leadership Team who pay their salary can't fix someone's behaviour, it's deeply unfair to expect a VA to.

If someone is constantly overloading themselves by taking on too much work and then letting people down, excellent diary support may help, but it isn't getting to the root of the problem. If they are behaving badly because they are too busy and just need some help, that's one thing. But you can't add organisational support to fix a person's poor behaviour. I have honestly been brought on by a leadership board that failed to manage their MD. Well, if you guys can't do it, how am I meant to in 20 hours a month? Be honest about what you are trying to fix and whether a VA is the right resource to do it. Or if resource is even the issue to be solved.

Do you have the time to bring a VA up to speed?

Do you have the time to recruit and onboard someone properly at this moment in your business and life, or would another point in the year get you off to a better start?

Getting a VA isn't an instant fix to getting your time back. It will, of course, in the long run, but there is an inevitable amount of time that you will need to invest in getting this project off the ground. If you do a poor job of bringing someone in, it will impact on what you get out of them. So be honest about your commitments.

Hold time in your diary well ahead of your VA joining to commit to them and to documenting your business. I'd also take a broad view of your diary to make sure that there aren't any huge deadlines, events, or projects that are going to fall at around the same time you need to find and onboard your new VA. If you want a VA to help with any of those things, then you are going to need to allow a decent chunk of time upfront for them to get in and start.

A Note on ADHD

Those with ADHD (Attention Deficit Hyperactivity Disorder) brains are amazing at their brilliance, laser focused and capable of delivering fantastic work, on time, on budget and wowing those around them. However, the things that are not their brilliance they really struggle to get excited about and to get themselves motivated to do. Fortunately, more and more folks with ADHD are discovering that working with a VA can be life changing.

I spoke to a number of business owners with ADHD while writing this book. People with ADHD can get overwhelmed by all the moving parts in both business and life and that overwhelm can lead to paralysis. Many business owners with ADHD are really frustrated by the things that don't get done even as they overachieve in many other areas of their work life. There's also a tendency not to "see" some things that would be very obvious to a neuro-typical person.

Outsourcing everything but your brilliance is even more critical for those whose brains work in this unique way – because unlike those of us who will (eventually) knuckle down and grumble through the things we find tedious, those with ADHD really find that challenging, so those things get left or overlooked. And if you are running a business, things like not sorting out your VAT return really can have some nasty consequences.

This is where the right VA can be a huge asset, scooping up things that are necessary but fall outside of your scope of interest and genius. A VA can also suggest systems and ways of working that might help make some of these tasks easier in the future. At the time of writing, there is even an Access to Work grant in the UK that some people can use to pay for some VA support. This is sometimes called a "work aide" as that seems to be a more understood term.

If you have ADHD it is worth finding a VA that has experience working with ADHD folks, as they will know what systems tend to work better for people with ADHD. ADHD comes in various forms and what works for one person may not work for another, so having that knowledge is vital.

Thanks to my conversations with business owners with ADHD, here are some top tips on how to make best use of VA support:

> **Ideas collation:** Ask your VA to be the keeper of all your great ideas without immediately leaping into action on all of them straight away. ADHD folks are frequently very creative and churn ideas out at a huge rate of knots, but they aren't

all things to follow up on. Or at least not without a second conversation.

Finishing and implementing ideas: You may want some of your ideas brought to life and that's where a VA can be a real boon. If you aren't a natural finisher of tasks, more the generator of inspiration, a VA can help you get into the processes and day to day repetition that isn't really your zone of genius.

Body Doubling: This is simply working together, usually on a video call. This can trigger the "mirror" neurons in your brain to focus as you watch others working. You may also choose to use calls with your VA to get short tasks done. Rather than chase a five-minute task needed to push a project forward, for example, a smart VA might use a catch-up call to say, "While we're talking, can you go into Dropbox and just add me to the Receipts folder". Doing it "live" is much easier for some people when it's a little task. You may also want to check out some online co-working sites like Flown (see resources).

Motivation: This can be tricky for ADHD folks in some areas. Having someone reframe a task or even nag you can make all the difference. Reminders are often wanted by ADHD clients even if they may silently roll their eyes and find it annoying. If you want to be reminded about things, ask your VA—and then don't be surprised when they do it! It may be that they need to explicitly say "you asked me to remind you about xxx" as they do.

Prioritisation: This is an excellent opportunity for collaboration with your VA. Between you, you can agree what needs doing and when. Your VA can also hold you accountable. This is absolutely something I do with my VA, Helen. Taken to a more granular level, you can have your VA help you plan your day and your week if it's helpful.

All those with ADHD I spoke to about working with VAs or other outsourced support said that it has been incredibly helpful for them. They are all very self-aware and have built solid relationships with their team by being really open about what works and what doesn't work for them.

(Another) Reality Check – Are you too much of a mess for a VA?

This is a moment for some self-examination.

To put it simply, if you are a born hot mess, even the most amazing VA in the world is not going to be able to make you organised. No VA can work miracles.

Many of our clients say to me "I'm so disorganised, it's carnage, I'm useless" but when you dig down into it, they are extremely competent, organised people who are just overwhelmed by sheer volume of work. They know what needs doing and by when, but they simply don't have enough hours in the day to get through it. The odd ball may drop once in a while when it gets really manic but by and large they keep afloat. It could just be done a lot less painfully if another pair of hands was helping, and it would give them more scope to do what they are brilliant at, rather than everything.

The contrast is someone who hasn't really got a grip on what needs doing. They can't prioritise. They rarely, if ever, make decisions about what to do and stick to it. They regularly miss deadlines or double book themselves. Meetings overrun, bills go unpaid until bailiffs' letters appear, and they often get fined for being late with tax payments. These types of people are extremely rare. And as they aren't able to manage themselves, they are unlikely to find a VA very helpful. (See the section on ADHD which may be applicable to some of these people in some specific life areas, even if they are totally on top of others.)

If you aren't able to manage yourself, then attempting to also manage another person is likely to be disastrous. Yes, a VA may help you knock a few things off the to do list, they may even teach you some systems and processes to help get organised. But if you don't keep up with them (and naturally chaotic people don't!) despite all good intentions, they just create more mess and more work and quite likely an extremely frustrated VA with a mountain of unfinished tasks because no one has responded to their queries.

Just like hiring a personal trainer can't make you thin and hiring a cleaner can't make you tidy, hiring a VA will not make you organised. Only you can do that. A VA relationship will involve effort on your part and a level of organisation at your end to make it work. No one is organised all the time. We all have the capacity for chaos and most of us have days where we feel totally out of control, and we forget things. That is completely normal. But if that is an ongoing experience and describes your life every day and you never force yourself to step back, breathe and look outside of the urgent pile, it's never going to end. And you will be a horrible client for a VA even if you are the loveliest person to walk the earth.

So how do you know which you are? Because in my experience there are actually very few people who fall into camp two. Especially those running a successful business, because clients rarely enjoy working with people who can't deliver on time. Here are some questions to test yourself for a bit of fun.

Test yourself - are you a hot mess? A Quick Quiz!

Client work:

a) Is always done and delivered on time (even if it might take a bit of midnight oil).

b) Is delivered on time 90% of the time.

c) Is sometimes delivered on time but they might have to chase me, or I might have to ask for extended deadlines. I'm pretty much behind and under pressure at all times.

My inbox:

a) Is largely under control. There are some things needing a response, but I know and understand what I need to do.

b) Is a bit behind. I have lots needing a reply and more needing to be filed away or sorted out and a load of things to unsubscribe from. It's a bit of a battle to keep on top of it.

c) Is a living nightmare. I have 80,000 unread messages, no real idea which need to be replied to, and suspect that some unread ones are now so old they are irrelevant.

I respond to emails:

a) Usually within 24 hours, but it might take two or three days if I'm travelling or under pressure or it isn't an urgent matter. People very rarely have to chase me for a reply.

b) Not as quickly as I would like, unless it's a client. It can take a week or two to get back to people that aren't clients as that always gets prioritised. Suppliers and contacts may need to chase me from time to time.

c) Occasionally. I get so many emails I don't even read them all, let alone reply. I am frequently being told "I sent you an email" and have no clue what people are talking about. I don't have a system; I just pick up the ones that look most urgent.

My days and weeks are:

    a) Mostly planned. I make sure I know what I need to get done and by when. Stuff comes up and derails my plans some days, so I have to move things or work late, but even though it is a massive list, I have a list.

    b) A bit patchy. I roughly know when I start work what I am going to do that day, but I don't plan it in advance, so sometimes I am caught out by deadlines approaching quicker than I thought.

    c) Mostly firefighting. My tasks are decided by whoever shouts loudest or happens to be in front of me. I have a mental list of things I want to get done but I never seem to get to them unless someone is actually waving it in my face.

My long-term planning is:

    a) In place. Maybe a bit optimistic given how busy I am, but I have a plan of where I want the business to be this year and clear steps on what needs doing to get to that point.

    b) Hit and miss. I have some targets but never seem to have the time to look at them and work out what I should be doing to hit them. Or I know full well what needs doing to hit them but anything "non-income based" just falls to the bottom of the list and a quiet day never seems to come along for me to do that kind of thing.

c) Non-existent. I don't have a long-term plan. I need to survive today without having a nervous breakdown (or giving one to those around me) and ideally until the weekend when I can treat myself to a massive gin and forget about another week of total carnage.

When I work with external suppliers, I:

a) Respond to any questions they have fairly promptly, deal with any problems as quickly as I can, and pay them on time.

b) Start out really well but can get distracted after a while and need to be chased for both input and possibly payment. Sorry!

c) Have to be chased 45 times for a response or answer to anything and am usually late paying as the invoice will have gone into my inbox of death so I'll probably not see it ever.

My invoices are:

a) Sent on time and chased in a timely fashion.

b) Usually sent more or less on time and I chase missing money sporadically.

c) Still waiting to be done six months after the work is complete.

How did you do?

Mostly A's

You are an organised person! Very organised indeed. If you are struggling to keep up with your beautifully created lists and goals it isn't because you are chaotic, it's because you have too much on. But you know exactly what needs to be done and by when and that is brilliant when it comes to outsourcing. Any VA will be delighted to have you as a client and between you you'll accomplish huge amounts.

Mostly B's

You are a normal human being doing their best in a crazy busy world. You do know what needs doing, though you may have said yes to too many things at once and are in danger of drowning a bit. You probably have days when you feel totally overwhelmed and as if you are disorganised, but likely you aren't disorganised at all, just swamped. A VA could certainly help you tame the task list and make life more manageable.

Mostly C's

Oh dear me! Bless you, your life is a bit of a hot mess, isn't it? Before you think about outsourcing you need to get a better grip on managing your own workday and getting some structure around how you prioritise. If you take on a VA at the moment, you will likely just drown them in stuff and never do anything with the things they send back because you are in too much chaos. If your life is this out of control, I would look at getting a decent coach to work with you first before anyone else, as that will be a better investment. But with a coach, as with a VA, you will need to make time and let them help you — which may mean feeling a bit more stressed in the short term.

So, are you ready for a VA?

If you answered mostly As and Bs, we can safely assume you will benefit from working with a VA. If you also worked your way through the questions in this chapter and have decided now is indeed the right time to hire (or want to plan for later), you're ready to get the low down on the kinds of assistants you could work with.

***

ACTION STEPS

1. Answer the questions posed in each header through this chapter. What do your answers tell you about whether or not now's the right time to hire?
2. Take the Quiz and confirm you're mostly As and Bs.
3. Look at your diary for the next few months. When would be a good time to find and onboard your new VA?

Three

What Kind of Assistant is Right for You?

"Someone who has your back, who understands your personality and your life and is there to protect you, is the single most important person you'll have in your business." Simon Sinek

If you've decided that you absolutely need and are ready for some support in your business, the next stage is looking at what support that might be. Should it be a Virtual Assistant, an employed Assistant (PA, or sometimes called EA depending on the specifics of the role), or something else altogether? If you make the wrong call early it can cost you time, money and a lot of wasted effort, so we're going to get into some depth in this chapter.

Both VAs and PAs support business owners and leaders so those leaders can spend their time on what's most crucial to their role. But whereas a VA is a freelancer who works for other companies besides yours, a PA (or EA) is an employee of your company who works (mostly) physically alongside you, and only for your company. There are a number of factors that will impact which kind of assistant is the right one for you. There is no single right answer – it depends on you and your business. I've counselled people that have got in touch with me for VA support to hire a PA instead on many occasions where it's a more cost-efficient option or there are other factors that make it a better choice. Conversely, I know many who have moved from a working with a PA to working with a VA as their needs have changed.

Location

This may be obvious but honestly you wouldn't believe how many times I have to point it out: Virtual Assistants by their very nature are virtual. They don't work in your office. They won't pop round to your house to pick up your receipts, they won't come and minute meetings live, and they won't meet for a coffee. That's a little black and white—I do know many VAs that will occasionally do all those things, but it's a bonus not an expectation. If any of those things are a non-negotiable, then you might consider that a PA would be a better option. You can hire someone that lives nearby and dictate where they work.

I know VAs that have worked out of Thailand, the rain forests in Ecuador, the mountains in Spain. In fact, it shouldn't really be obvious where they're working at all, they just get on with it.

The reason VAs are cost effective is that we switch seamlessly between clients with a flick of a timesheet. If we are physically travelling between them, that efficiency is totally lost. If we are working onsite for a client, that entire time is billed because we can't work for anyone else while we're onsite. So, suddenly you find it's not as cost effective because you are paying for trips to the kettle or a quick loo break. We are much more cost effective in our own offices!

VAs have been around for decades and have been quietly and efficiently getting stuff done without much fanfare. During COVID 19 the rest of the world caught on to the idea that remote working is not only possible, but actually pretty efficient. And boy how we VAs laughed as you all had to suss out Zoom calls ("you're on mute, Steve!"), setting up home offices so you didn't break your spine sat on a dining room chair, and "building relationships remotely". We've been doing it for years. It works. Working remotely is still work. In addition, it is totally possible to build a fabulous relationship with someone you have never met in person. I mean, I wouldn't recommend it for marriage, but for VAs and clients, with time and effort it works.

There's one other clear-cut circumstance where a remote VA isn't going to work very well: if you have a paper-based business. Some businesses, because of their regulatory needs, must still use old-school honest to goodness A4 in piles. And that is going to be tricky to manage for a VA. I have seen it done with a combination of PO boxes and storage, but it isn't easy, and I'd certainly be concerned about physically storing client data on my premises. Moving it between places by post or courier isn't ideal either. So, if part or all of the work you do involves a lot of paper and it isn't possible to move it online, you will probably be better off hiring a PA who can come to you.

Conversely, you can employ a PA who works remotely if you don't have an office. They are simply a home-based employee. And when you hire them, you can specify that you want them to be in the office, two days a week, once a month or five days a week. With an employee you can decide where and when you want them to work.

Physical safety

Just a note on safety. You wouldn't believe how many times strange men have asked me to come and meet them at their home office about work when I have just met them online. Given that (presently at least) the majority of VAs are female, please consider how they might feel about coming to your place of work if it isn't a professional office with other people. You know you're not an axe murderer, but they have no way of knowing that at all.

Would you be happy if your wife, sister, daughter went off to meet someone they have only met through LinkedIn on their own? Quite likely not. It isn't appropriate to expect a lone female to come to you having never met you before. Any initial in person meetings should be done in a public place, a coffee shop or co-working space or similar. It may not be as convenient for you, but it's the right call.

Office management and real-life visitors

If you have an office, what is its function? Does it ever see a client in person? Is there an absolute need for someone to be there that isn't you or one of your team? If you host meetings and events in the office, it probably makes sense to have an assistant onsite with you to meet and greet and help things run smoothly. But if your reception room is non-existent, don't hire someone to sit in a chair and greet the air all day. And if your office phone only rings rarely, it's not hard these days to add a forwarding option to a mobile or use a call answering service or a VOIP system (A VOIP phone number is a service delivered over the internet rather than a phone line and can be used in any location).

If your office is busy, do you need an extra person there for all or only part of the work? A hybrid solution of an employed person and a VA can work well if there is the volume of work to justify two roles. Depending on your need you might employ a receptionist or an office manager who coordinates all in-person needs. And on top you might have a VA who purely does diary management. Why, you might say, can the receptionist or office manager not do the diary as well? Maybe they can. It will depend both on the amount of work and the complexity as well as the person you hire. But if your diary requires a highly skilled EA with amazing credentials that employed would likely earn £80K, she's unlikely to want to commute to Hammersmith and earn £30K. And if you hire someone on £30K, they are highly unlikely to have the skills and experience that your top-level VA has to manage a complex diary. You pick your person for the job. Or you pick multiple people and divide and conquer.

Grown-ups and chasing people round the office

Have you ever worked with anyone who absolutely can't be on time for anything if their life depends on it? Someone you've threatened to put a tracker on because they are never where they are meant to be? Someone who gets so engrossed in their conversation or work that time becomes irrelevant? We all have, to some extent. But those who live like that all the time are sometimes ably managed by saint-like PAs whose main function is to be a human alarm clock and physically drag them between meetings.

As you can tell, I'm not a lover of this role! But some people need it and value it. Having to think about time as well as their brilliance isn't an option. That's just how they are built. To mitigate this, they have a PA who comes and tells them when the cab has arrived for the airport or gently sticks their head into a meeting and says that the next visitor is waiting.

If you need that—and I mean really need that, not just lose track of time occasionally as we all do, but genuinely cannot finish a meeting on time and move to the next one—you need a PA. You need someone in person waving at you. That cannot be done by Zoom or email, you'll leave a VA wanting to murder you remotely. Hire a PA. Hire a really, really tolerant PA who never needs to have a lunch break unless you are safely ensconced in a meeting.

On-tap support

There are some roles where an EA would quite rightly always be by the side of their Exec. In meetings, travelling with them and more or less available 24/7. Those are roles for extraordinarily well paid EAs and are few and far between in the UK, usually reserved for FTSE 100 CEOS, celebrities and high-net-worth individuals.

Thinking about your diary, realistically, how many times a week do things change the same day? It may feel like a lot but likely it isn't as many as you think, or they are speedy little switches that you just do yourself. People tend to over-estimate how fast paced their diary is because life feels fast paced and intense due to the sheer volume of meetings. Likely there aren't that many meetings that change frequently.

There are some people who need support all the time. They need a dedicated person who is always available at the end of the phone to answer a question. If you are one of those people who regularly need to wipe a whole day of meetings and reschedule them on the day, maybe you do need someone in a PA role. Or maybe some longer-term planning would be the answer.

VAs are not ideal if you need an instant response to things. We have multiple clients, we go to meetings, we might spend a Tuesday afternoon once a month abseiling down buildings. All of which means you might have to wait a few hours for a reply. There are some roles that are so complicated and fast paced that you may need a dedicated person. But you'd be surprised how rare that is. It may be that you're used to having that level of support but on reflection decide that you don't need it. We support managing partners in incredibly busy multi-million-pound businesses, and they manage just fine with a VA. Part of it is a mindset thing, part of it is need.

Since occasional last-minute changes are inevitable, what happens during those last-minute changes is key.

Client messages their VA at 13.30

"Hiya, my 13.00 is wildly overrunning, can you let Arif know?" Arif being booked at 14.00.

If the VA doesn't respond, they're maybe in a meeting with another client or head down on a complex task with their notifications off, the client will sort it themselves.

If you cannot fathom the concept of letting someone know you're running late yourself on occasion, you need a PA.

Sharing

Whilst we do switch between clients that doesn't mean we don't absolutely value you and your work—we do. A good VA will always make you feel valued. We just have to value others as well.

By their nature, VAs support multiple clients. I know some of our clients find it quite fascinating that they could be sharing their VA with a gardener or a lawyer in any given day. It fries their brain a little and reminds them how flexible and adaptable we VAs are.

Your VA having multiple clients can be a huge benefit to you too – think of all the things we learn working in so many different businesses, including new ideas for software, suppliers, event locations.

Professional VAs are always very careful to ensure client confidentiality. We absolutely wouldn't share any details about you or your business with any other client and vice-versa. Our contracts will typically have non-disclosure elements and most VAs are more than happy to also sign your NDA if you think additional clauses are needed.

But in general, you do need to be comfortable with the fact that your VA is not solely dedicated to you. You have no control over who else they work with. If that makes you feel a bit twitchy, then you'll need to employ someone.

Substitutes and associates

When you take on a VA, you are contracting with another business. Which means the VA, as a business owner, has some control over the work, including who does that work.

As Annabel Kaye covers in more detail on her Bonus Chapter, letting your VA send a substitute (usually an associate) is really key in differentiating them from a "worker" in UK tax terms so it's important that you are open to this.

Flexibility

VAs are freelance. Whilst we might work 9-5 (and we might not) that doesn't mean we are **available** 9-5 for you at a moment's notice.

Some VAs work at irregular times. Some might be in a different time zone. And for most clients, as long as the work gets done, that's fine. We generally don't tell people when we're doing their work. You don't get four hours every Wednesday or whatever. It's more fluid than that. Which is better for you as we'll be checking in more regularly, even if it's 10 minutes a day. Flexibility makes for a great VA client. As VAs we're pretty agile and fast paced so having a client that works that way too helps us.

Can you be flexible about when tasks get done, as long as all communication milestones and deadlines are met? If so, a VA is a good match. If not, a PA is probably better for you.

Volume of hours

I once had a conversation with a prospective client who had a team of people that she needed to source support for. I think there were about 20 of them, plus two team leads who needed a bit more support than their direct reports.

She wanted full diary management, support with diary strategy, complex travel arrangements, and expense receipts for 22 people. And she thought that one VA could do that. And quite possibly she thought that one VA could do it in 20 hours a month for £10 an hour. I mean, deluded didn't even begin to describe it. VAs are good, but we aren't miracle workers! No one employed PA could manage that volume of work. But several VAs could—I suggested five. Much to her horror. I mean maybe one PA could support two team leads and give a little ad hoc travel support to the team now and again. But full diary management and the rest for 22 people? Hardly. In that circumstance, a team of VAs would be brilliant because you could flex up and down as needs changed, but she wouldn't hear it, she wanted a Virtual Assistant. Singular, and no room to flex on the tasks taken on. I suggested that perhaps we weren't the right option.

If you need a lot of hours, that should be spread across multiple VAs, and that is actually a really good thing! You get built in holiday and illness cover when you have a team of two or more. One VA can't do it all, not only because we're not superhuman, but also because we'd have to give you all our working hours. It's bad practice to have just one client. For IR35 purposes, for business security purposes, it is rarely done. We usually look after three to eight clients at a time; my survey of VAs had the most common number at six.

At some point when you are using up a lot of VA hours, especially on a one-to-one basis, there may come a time when it's more cost-effective to employ someone full-time. Or there may come a time when you need more hours than your VA or VA team has available. We look at how to handle this gracefully in Chapter Seven.

Costs

The hourly rate of VAs and PAs is not easily comparable. VA rates are higher than an employee's hourly rate or a temp's rate; like all freelancers, we cover many of our costs ourselves so that is built into our hourly rate.

Here are some of the things you pay for when you employ someone and versus hiring a freelance VA service.

	Employees	VAs
Bonus	Maybe	No
Sick pay	Yes	No
Parental leave	Yes	No
National Insurance	Yes	No
Tax	Yes	No
Holiday pay	Yes	No
Equipment – laptop, phone	Yes	No, unless you choose to for security purposes
Software	Yes	Some *
Breaks	Yes	No
Pension	Yes	No
Office furniture	Yes	No
Insurance	Yes	No
Training and development	Yes	No – unless system specific
Time spent faffing	Yes	No

* A VA will have the right kit and software to cover the basics, but you may well have to pay for extra licenses on MS 365 plus a CRM or similar, if you use them, to add them as a user

Cost comparison for an employee versus a freelance VA

As an extremely rough guide, if a VA covers for a fulltime, office-based PA for 40 hours a week, we do it in "VA time" in around 20 hours a week. That's in large part because you are only paying for very focused time on the clock. No trips to the kitchen or popping to Costa.

This isn't an exact science, of course, as PA jobs differ wildly, but because of the way we bill, we're exceedingly efficient.

Response time

We've already touched on the kind of support you need, whether you need someone available at all moments or not.

Realistically, you need to understand how VA response times work and make adjustments with any VA you take on to ensure everyone is happy.

Some VAs will give an expected response time or a turnaround time on their tasks. If they do a particular kind of work, this might be quite accurate. But while all tasks or emails should be looked at within that response time, that doesn't mean they need doing in that time. Bigger projects may not be done that quickly. With longer-term projects you'd expect to be getting regular updates. If you haven't agreed the milestones for a check in, then you should have an idea where progress is – either with specific updates or by checking a shared project management tool. An ideal VA job is a blend of quick tasks and then this more ongoing or repetitive work that can be done over the course of a few days, weeks or even months. We have the brains to prioritise what is important, and we'll make a call based on that and our current capacity.

If that all feels too hands off for you, you may well be better with someone who is employed. When you hire someone, their entire working day is at your disposal and if you want to control the priorities it is only your work that is in the mix. If you want them to move something up the list, it's your list to manage as you see fit.

Similarly, you may feel all your tasks are urgent tasks. I will always seriously question anyone who says all their tasks are "I need this ASAP" tasks rather than "add it to the list when you have time" tasks. But if that truly is the case, then you need a PA rather than a VA so that you have full control over how they spend their working hours to deliver you what they need.

Micromanaging

Talking of managing as you see fit...let's talk about micromanaging.

Virtual Assistants are smart, can-do kind of folk. We enjoy the variety of our working lives and the autonomy to get the job done the best way we know how. And we have the skills and experience to do that because we've learnt from our past employed careers and from working with other clients.

If you are the kind of person who wants every task done their way every time, a VA may not be the right solution for you. It is much easier to watch how someone does something and check it is the way you want it when they are sat in the same room as you. And if that's how your business runs, then an onsite PA would be more appropriate.

A VA also won't be cost effective for you if you like to micromanage. There will be an inordinate amount of back and forth if you aren't able to relinquish some control. Every back and forth is costing you money because it is time spent. If you've been told that you are a micromanager, you'll need to do a little self-reflection before you hire a VA. Working on the clock, we get expensive if everything has to be checked 17 times before it's signed off. I recall one client where her grip on her diary was so tight, I couldn't book in anything without her agreement. Which made the whole exercise pointless. She'd copy me in on an email to book in a 30-minute call with someone. It wasn't especially urgent or important, but she would insist on knowing what slots I was going to offer and approving them before they were sent, for a not very important meeting in a diary that wasn't especially complex. It was madness. We parted ways very soon afterwards.

What is your communication preference?

Some people really communicate better in person. That's just a preference. If you know that you aren't comfortable with purely remote communication and need to eyeball someone in real life on a regular basis, then you may well be better with an in-person employed PA that can work part time hours in your office.

It's not an "assistant" at all…

With the rise in talented VAs, the number of things they can do has grown. With this comes a slight tendency for clients to think a VA is the solution to every problem. And sometimes it isn't.

Sometimes, you need to pay for a specialist.

This is a weird and slightly blurry line but if, for example, you were rebranding and then going out to market with your new brand with a relaunch and a whole host of other marketing, you would want an expert on the case. Or probably several. With the best will in the world, a £40 per hour VA isn't going have the same level of experience as a full-service marketing and branding agency.

I talk to prospects about social media work very frequently. If you want a VA to put some posts up on LinkedIn, research articles to post, maybe (and it really is maybe because it is by no means a universal skill) draft the odd blog for you, then a VA that has some knowledge of social media would be fine. If that is where your budget is, just enough that people don't think you're dead, great, go with a VA with social media on their skills list.

However, if you want your social media to bring you in new clients, you have goals and targets for it, and you need it to be impactful, then you'll need a full social media strategy created for you. And that's not a 'couple of hours' task. There are some VAs that will do this, usually at a package price, but for this level, you'd really need a social media specialist. And that would be my search term, rather than VA. Do bear in mind that you're not going to get a social media strategy, Google Ads, or complex SEO at VA rates because the skills and expertise that it takes to create this plan and implement it are many years in the making.

Similarly, VAs are not an alternative to an accountant. Yes, some of us do bookkeeping, but there are some things an accountant does that even a specialist VA doesn't do.

As a caveat, when you first start up and funds are low, it might be the right call to get a VA that is good at whatever skill it is you are missing. That's good enough for now. Just be aware that you get what you pay for, and you may need to manage your expectations when you pay £40 an hour for a VA rather than £80 per hour for a podcast engineer or a video editor.

Has this given you some food for thought on what kind of assistant might be the right fit for you? If it turns out that you need a PA, you will still find some later sections in the book useful, in particular the onboarding and working better together sections in Chapter Seven.

If a VA still feels like the right option, then onward! Let's get into the world of the VA.

***

ACTION STEPS

1. Go through each heading in this chapter and decide if a VA or PA is more suitable for you in that category.

2. Tally them up to see who wins. (If you're feeling fancy, you could even make yourself a little spreadsheet with the headings in column A, VA in column B, and PA in column C. Make Excel do the tally for you.) I love a spreadsheet and I won't judge.

Four

What a VA can Really Do for You

To summarise what we know so far: A Virtual Assistant is someone who works remotely to support another business. For the context of this book, we're going to assume that all VAs are self-employed freelancers. In other words, by working with a VA you are buying a service from another business. Some VAs may be employed by an agency, but the agency you contract to will still be another company, rather than your own employee. There are some bigger firms out there, like KPMG, that have what they call Virtual Assistant roles, but these are employed roles and might be better described as "Remote PA". We're also focusing in this book on the UK VA industry and not the global one, for reasons I will go into later.

By working virtually, a VA can support multiple clients at any one time and most of us have anything between three and eight clients simultaneously, depending on the volume and frequency of the work that those clients need.

What working with a VA is like

A VA can pick up many tasks and can also be a "second brain" for you, helping you keep on top of your To Do list and projects. Whilst you can have a Virtual Assistant that just does odd bits of work here and there, the real value is having one that works alongside you every week. They get to know you and the business and can then really start to make a difference to your working life by freeing up your time. Here are some of the ways that can work.

The hand of the king

Or the power behind the throne, depending on your nerd-o-meter. We drink and we know things, as Tyrion from Game of Thrones might say.

This can be a really strange concept for those not in this position, but we assistants (whether real life or virtual) really love seeing our clients succeed. That is where we get our kicks. It does take a certain type of personality but when you find one, you'll know.

We are happy to beaver away in the background getting things done and supporting (mostly, there's the odd flamboyant VA out there that you can't miss!). We have the ear of the "King" or "Queen" and often are responsible for passing on their wishes to others, communicating on their behalf and being a strategic advisor on occasion.

We provide support. This doesn't make us subservient. Our work is part of your role –

you're the ideas person and we scoop those up and follow through. It's a different kind of role and takes a certain kind of person to not be the one on stage doing the dancing. We'll be at the back (in our home offices) with a clipboard making notes and checking that the catering van has arrived on time.

I know that I've "made it" with a client when they get in touch with good news, not because I need to know it to action anything, but because they know I'm interested, and that I care. I want to celebrate with them. I'm also happy to commiserate with them when things haven't gone so well.

Moral support

It can be really lonely doing your job, can't it?

I know. I run a business too. Before I got my first VA I used to have to vent to the dogs and they're terrible listeners with a tendency to wander off mid-sentence and fart as they go.

Whether you're running a business of one, four or 200, being you can be lonely because you can't always talk to everyone about what's going on. It isn't appropriate to have a vent about a team member to another team member. You might have a board that you can talk to, even a peer, but they are no doubt insanely busy as well and it's not the best use of their time, satisfying as it might be for you both, to do a 15 minute whinge about Kelly resigning, Paulo demanding to know why he didn't get a promotion when he's only been in the role for ten minutes and Sarah ballsing up a client event, which means you need to go in and sort it out and dear God haven't you got enough to sodding do?

But your VA can be an outlet for that. And many of us are. At one point I Googled what marriage guidance counsellors charge per hour because I felt I was undercharging with a particular client!

In all seriousness, as external suppliers, VAs are ideally placed to hear confidential information. We're not mates with Paulo and think we should probably tell him he's pissed you off. We don't have any personal skin in the game if someone has made a mistake or resigned or is going through a tough patch with a client. We're one step removed. We can hear the download, letting you get it off your chest and then move on with your day.

Most PAs when employed have this incredibly confidential role. I recall many times as a PA hearing things about colleagues I would rather I hadn't, but it was the nature of the role. You just have to keep your mouth shut and carry on. Discretion is everything as a PA, and VAs too are also nothing if not discreet. Typically, part of our contract carries a non-disclosure clause and most VAs I know are more than happy to sign an NDA on top if you want us to. We didn't go into business to steal your ideas or your IP, but we understand that trust takes some time to build up.

Being one step removed from an organisation is extremely helpful for us to not get too emotionally attached. I sometimes have a little saying I mutter to myself when internal client politics get a bit wild: "Not my circus, not my monkeys". Things that perhaps impact the organisation and those that are employed don't have quite the same effect on us. For example, the agency I run has worked with many companies now that rely on funding to keep going. Often the VA will know when the money is running out and whether there are likely to be issues getting a renewal. As an employee, that's someone's whole job. That would be a very unsettling piece of information to have. As a VA, it will make us a bit sad, especially if we like the client and the team, that the work is likely to come to an end. But as we all have multiple clients it isn't going to be as awful for us as an employee who will be made redundant. We have other things to keep us afloat until we fill that gap.

Sounding board

For solopreneurs, VAs may be the only other person in their business, and therefore the only one that they can talk to in order to think through ideas. This is not to be underestimated! When your business is just you, it's easy to get stuck in a rut. Having someone to talk to and bounce ideas off can refresh and reinvigorate you, especially when your VA can then move forward with some of those ideas to test them out and see if they are going to be runners.

Talking out loud can also help you organise your ideas and brainstorm new ideas. When you talk out loud, you are forced to turn your ideas into something coherent as you speak so the listener can understand, which makes you make sense of what is in your head. Questions, or a lack of understanding from the listener, are a prompt to re-jig that thought or explain it more cogently.

I used to have a quick call every week with one client to catch up on projects, questions, anything coming up in the week ahead, but there was one day she talked at me for a full 40 minutes. Calls are, of course, billable. Much of it was quite complex website techy stuff that I didn't really understand. Some was more sales orientated and I interjected an "uh huh" at points just so she knew I was alive and paying attention. Occasionally I had a question or a clarification. At the end of the call, she apologised and said, "I'm so sorry I just talked at you for the whole call. But saying it all out loud like that, I know what I need to do now. Have you got anything for me?" No apologies needed. That's a great use of my time. She might have spent a day trying to work that out on paper, but talking it out, even to me who really hadn't much of a clue, was what was needed to nail it in 40 minutes.

Second brain

I often describe VAs as a second brain. They don't just take a task from you and return it, they actively manage projects and have their finger on the pulse of what's going on.

Holding in your head everything that needs to get done for clients, for internal folk, for prospects, for the kids, for your partner and for your friend's birthday next week is a lot. Even if you use a task management system so it's all written down, it's still in your head as well because it's on you to remember to look at the task system and then do it. This mental load is exhausting if it's all yours. A VA will take some of these things off you AND help you remember what needs doing.

One client used to call me "the nagging witch of his prospect list", which I took to be a supreme compliment! What he meant was that I'd remind him that he said "I really should have a coffee with Tom" if I hadn't seen that appear in his diary anywhere or any emails asking Tom for a coffee. And if I hadn't heard anything following a proposal going out, I'd ask "any news, do we need to chase that in a few days" or whatever. Let your brain have a break and share some responsibility with a VA as the person who makes sure things happen and chases if they don't.

There are some nifty tech tools these days that make taking on this role really easy and we all love to use them so we can be the one that remembers. You don't need to do it all.

My VA Helen is amazing at this. I am, as you'd expect, pretty organised. It's what I do. But that doesn't mean that I can't get overloaded and have things fall through the cracks. I've passed her some of the things that were frequently on what I call my "guilt list". Things I really should do but for whatever reason I seem to find particularly hard to get around to. They are no longer on my guilt list—because Helen does them. It's mostly checking things that I have niggles about and giving me a super-fast summary on anything I actually need to worry about. Knowing that I don't need to think about it is such a relief. And some of those checks she does for me, she'll say, "I noticed this, so I have asked XX to fix it" and I don't even need to get involved. Magic. Helen will also work with me on projects and she's very good at tactfully saying "what is the next step to move this forward" when clearly, I was meant to do something on a project and didn't!

I do have to do my part in this though. If I do something, I have to tell her. Or update our shared system so she knows it's done. You'll have to do the same with your VA. There's nothing more annoying than a list of To Dos that isn't accurate because the person you're supporting did three of them and forgot to tell you or tick them off centrally or copy you on the emails so you'd be aware.

One client beautifully described his VA as "just the right side of pushy". Exactly. We'll support you, but sometimes the support you need is a gentle reminder—or a firm shove.

Meeting support

Meetings breed actions I find, and you might want to have a VA join you in some of your meetings to take notes and potentially take some of your actions away. Some VAs are happy to support you in meetings, some are not. Whilst having someone join a meeting and take notes for you is an absolute joy and a weight off your mind, it is a) not everyone's cup of tea, so don't assume your VA will take this on unless you have asked when you hired them and b) can be a chunk of time that quickly adds up.

If you have a team meeting every Monday for an hour, your VA will need to either commit to being there every week (and that may not be possible) or you'll have to be OK with recording the session for them to listen to later or be OK with them sending a substitute. Whilst recording a meeting sounds great, it only takes someone who mumbles and a super-fast speaker with a thick accent (or eating an apple, I kid you not, I was once trying to fathom what someone was saying while they were eating an apple!) for that to become tricky work. You may find you have a chunk of questions and "I couldn't hear that bit" to manage.

Your VA may ask you if you're happy for them to record the meeting they are minuting as a back-up when they are typing up. You may or may not be OK with this, if you are then they need to have an agreed process for deleting those recordings fully once the notes are finalised.

You'll need to allow about the same length of time as the meeting itself to write up for an actions-type informal meeting and about three times the meeting length if you want a full transcript or a more in depth set of notes. If it's a very formal meeting where there are going to be multiple iterations before the minutes are signed off by the Chair, that's a lot of time and effort and therefore a considerable investment on your part.

These days you can get Teams or Zoom to create you a transcript of a meeting. In my experience they are totally hilarious and well worth a read, but probably useless as a record of the meeting. There are better apps to use (Otter.ai is a favourite) but a transcript is a long read if you only need action points pulling out. And you may not want sensitive meetings recorded at all for obvious reasons.

There are meetings and there are meetings. For a 30 minute internal team meeting "please record the actions and a short overview" is one thing, but to officially minute a board meeting or an Annual General Meeting, particularly if you're in a regulated industry or have very formal committee meetings, this is complex and a fairly specialist skill so you'll likely need to hire specifically for that. Minuting is a task that everyone assumes a VA can and will do but, in my experience, there are a handful of people that love it and are experts and the rest of us avoid it like the bubonic plague. Remember that when you hire a VA it's not like having an employee –

as a PA we may have had to do minutes as part of our job, like it or loathe it, as a VA we can say "no thank you", unless we signed up to it upfront.

Myths and Legends about VAs

Ahead of looking in depth at how VAs operate, let me dispel one or two myths and legends about VAs.

I hope by now we've established that we're neither Siri nor Alexa. We are in fact real humans. Here are some other preconceptions that I've come across over the years.

You answer the phone

No, no we don't!

Very few VAs offer a phone answering service because it's a royal pain in the wotsit. If clients are paying us to answer all their calls, we can't be in a meeting with anyone else, in the loo, in the park with the kids. And the phone may never ring. So how the hell do you charge for that? It's a messy task, so most VAs don't go there.

There are specialist phone answering services or agencies that manage calls for multiple clients and are set up to do so. They have teams so that someone is always free to get the call and they will have the right equipment to handle calls and pass them around as needed. Some will also do some light scheduling or customer service as well. If you need phone calls managing, those types of agencies are much more cost effective than paying a VA to do it. Several times I've known these call answering services work alongside a VA, sending on messages to the VA so they can then deal with the request and call back as needed.

You're available 24/7

Oh hell no again! I turn into a pumpkin at 6PM and woe betide any client that calls me after that. There had better be a very urgent crisis.

VAs choose our hours to suit us. And sometimes that might mean you get an email at 9PM or at a weekend, but that does not mean it is ok to call at 9PM. Or expect a reply before Monday. We're not a 24-hour hotline. Most VAs will tell you what their core hours are, though they may or may not pick up calls during those hours as they could be on the clock, elsewhere or busy. Some VAs are exceedingly strict with their devices and will literally turn everything off outside working hours. Others of us are a little more fluid, but no one is impressed by a client that routinely interrupts our lives outside of work.

If you travel a lot and are likely to need someone that occasionally has to deal with an out of hours crisis as you find yourself stranded in an airport in a snowstorm, it's as well to check how your VA handles this. Some simply won't - their time outside of work is valuable to them and they protect it. Others will but it's charged at a higher rate.

Also, it's worth noting that your definition of an emergency may not be our definition of an emergency. If we sent you all the information about your trip on Tuesday but you didn't read it before Sunday, the day of travel, it is not our problem if you now want something changed on Sunday morning. You had three full working days to check that. Don't wreck my Sunday because you've now decided you'd rather have a hotel closer to the airport. Tell me that Wednesday, Thursday or Friday. I did my bit in time, you need to hold up your end of the bargain.

VAs aren't as good as PAs

Obviously, you'd expect me to disagree here but actually I'm going with an "it depends". I've met some really awful PAs before! I mean terrible. Lazy, slapdash, and unresponsive. And I've also met some VAs that are world-class at what they do. And vice-versa. I've been both a PA and VA and I've met and worked with a lot of both. The work that PAs and VAs do is invaluable to the organisation that they support. And as with most roles, you get those that excel and those that do not.

It's largely down to the individual and what you hire them for.

What I would say is that it can be quite easy for a mediocre or even fairly terrible PA to hide in a big company for a very long time, doing the bare minimum and not being properly managed or brought up to speed, much less being fired. Their peers will know that they are awful. Probably people will avoid giving them things to do because they don't follow through. But support staff can be a strange area of a business as they aren't the ones doing the business of the business, they aren't consultants or lawyers or marketers and as such, the performance management of them can be hit and miss. Underperformance can go undetected and unmanaged for a long time when you aren't delivering the core service of the business.

A terrible VA can't go undetected, you just give them notice and get a new one. And a bad VA will eventually realise as contracts come to an end without being renewed, time and time again, that maybe they are the problem. Clients won't stick with poor VAs. And they don't even need to give a reason; it's not like an employee where you must manage them out. You simply say "I don't need you after next month" and they are gone. Unless they ask for feedback, they won't ever know that you got sick of the mistakes, the incessant typos, and all the things you had to chase them on that they forgot to do.

When you look for a VA it's worth asking how long their longest client relationship is. It's a red flag if they have been freelancing for years but haven't had a client partnership last longer than six months. I'd be wanting to know why. This is assuming they aren't purely project based. But even then, I'd expect some repeat business even if it's in fits and starts.

A good VA with the right background is effectively an amazing EA or PA, they just work in a different way. Our team of VAs often work alongside PAs or EAs in a company and to the outside world you wouldn't know the difference. In fact, we love working with PAs and EAs in a business because they will have got stuff organised and they'll know everything about everything, which means we have someone hugely knowledgeable to ask.

Many VAs have amazing experience from previous jobs, potentially they are graduates, ex-lawyers, ex-project managers. I even know one with an MBA!

Anyone can be a VA

I heard this so much I wrote my last book as a kind of reality check for people who were considering it. Much like coaching and counselling, anyone can call themselves a VA. Got a laptop, broadband, want some extra cash? Be a VA. A few years ago, there really was an article in a UK newspaper that more or less said this. Every VA I know that takes their business and their career seriously was incandescent with rage for a fortnight at this god-awful bit of journalism. I think it was the Daily Mail so, you know, no one is expecting quality or accuracy, but honestly it was bad. I got so many messages from people thinking that they could earn big bucks being a VA as a "side-hustle" (I hate that term almost as much as "mumpreneur") alongside their day job as a hairdresser or a bricklayer or whatever. You know, to get some extra cash for Christmas.

No, not anyone can be a VA.

Actually, not true. Anyone can be a VA. Not everyone can be a **good** VA. A good VA has many years (probably ten or even twenty-plus years) in the working world and knows how to get stuff done.

Whilst not every VA comes from a PA background, most will have transferable skills whether that's administration or project management, events coordination or account management. That's the bit that you're selling as a VA, you're just doing it freelance. If you don't have those skills and experience to sell, what are you offering people?

Good VAs are supremely organised and can help others get organised too. Competent with a multitude of systems and software, they can seamlessly adapt to whichever client they are working on and quite likely suggest ways things can be improved.

High level VAs are amazing communicators, able to build relationships over email, Zoom and Chat with ease and humour. Most VAs are happy to work independently with minimal supervision. People who like the tiniest details on every last thing and need to ask their client ten times a day don't tend to be successful VAs.

VAs have to be tech savvy. Even non-tech VAs have to be confident with different software across different clients because no one is going to be holding your hand showing you how to open someone else's calendar in Google. If a VA doesn't know it and asks their client, they look like an idiot. So VAs have to accept that they'll spend some of their own time learning the basics on the most popular systems. VAs rarely get paid to learn, since we're not employees. You either know it, or you go learn it off the clock without bothering anyone except YouTube.

As you see, not everyone is an ideal VA candidate. It takes dedication, organisation, tenacity, skills, experience and confidence to embrace a freelance VA role.

A VA will know what I want already

I often used to joke that some people thought PAs had Mystic Meg level psychic powers. It's much the same as being a VA.

An established VA will have all the skills and experience to do what is needed, but they won't know you. They won't know your business. You are a special and distinctive person! You will have your preferred ways of working, your own style and things that are unique to you. And we won't know these unless you tell us, because everyone we work with is different and we are not psychic.

As you read earlier, you will need to spend time with your VA for them to get up to speed. That is a given. It will take more time upfront. And you will need to commit regular time to your VA so that they can continue to support you. At Personally Virtual we suggest 30 minutes a week for a catch-up call, that can sometimes go down to 15 once things are running smoothly but there will be interactions outside of this.

A quarter of the VAs I surveyed had fired a client because they were poor communicators and had to be constantly chased. They didn't respond to emails, they stood the VA up for scheduled calls and it's frustrating. Even after five years supporting someone there will still be things we need to discuss with them. Decisions we can't make without their input, priorities we need to check. It's deeply frustrating for us as we just want to help. So, if you can't imagine a scenario where you can find ten minutes a day to communicate with your VA, this is going to be an issue.

We know you're busy, that's why we're here. But we can't work in a vacuum and we're not psychic!

If you won't reply to us, we can't physically track you down and drag you into a meeting room to ask you questions. If you're the blocker to the VA getting things done, that isn't their fault. Please don't say "Oh I had a VA, it didn't work" if you only replied to one in ten of their emails and missed more calls than you made. That wasn't a VA problem, that was a you problem. Own it and don't make another VA's life a misery until you're sure you can do better next time.

VAs are cheap

Certainly, working with a VA is a very cost-effective way of bringing support into your business. Compared to the outlay of bringing a permanent employee onboard, hiring a freelance VA or bringing in an agency is going to cost you less.

It's worth remembering though that freelance rates are not the same as employee rates. An hourly rate for a freelancer will always be more than the equivalent employed role because freelancers are paying for their own tax, National Insurance, computer equipment and allowing in their rate for time off for holidays, sickness etc.

In terms of rates, you'll get what you pay for. Just as there are levels for employees, there are levels for freelancers. You won't get a VA that can help you run your business if you're paying the lowest rate out there. A top end C Suite EA or private EA could potentially earn a salary of £60,000 - £80,000. I have even seen £120,000 per annum, although that is exceptional. Those highly skilled and experienced ex-EAs are not going to be freelancing for £20 an hour. You might get an admin VA for that, but I don't know any generalist VAs that charge less than £30 an hour. And I know a few exceptional specialists that charge up to £95 an hour. If you want to pay £15 an hour, you'll have to employ someone. That rate just won't cover anyone to work as a freelance VA in the UK. If people are willing to work at a very low rate that tells me that they are inexperienced, and I'd be concerned that they aren't paying for the things they should, like insurance, proper equipment and software, to keep their business and yours safe.

How a VA Operates

Whilst all VAs are different and will have their own ways of working, I want to give you a little look under the covers. A sneak peak, if you will, so that when you're talking to your potential VAs you know what you're talking about. Knowing your stuff upfront will mean your conversations can move more quickly to the specifics rather than your meetings being taken up getting you up to speed on an overview. Having this understanding will give you some background in why VAs may ask for certain things and how it's going to work for you, as a client, on a day-to-day basis.

We're part of the team (but not)

Being a freelancer in a business is a strange thing. In many ways we are part of the team. Sometimes we're the only team! But we aren't fully in the team because we have other places to be as well, mentally if not physically.

However, very often to the people you interact with, and we interact with it won't be apparent that we are anything other than a part of your business. Most VAs will work with an email address that you provide. This not only looks more professional, but it is also much more secure as well, as all the log ins you provide can use that email and you then have a much tighter control on all the data that you are sharing.

We will interact with others in your business and outside just as any member of the team would and you email us or send us messages on Teams or Slack just like you would anyone else. We just won't necessarily be there all day to pick things up.

Billable hours

Most (but not all) VAs work with billable time. A little bit like lawyers, if you have ever seen how they bill.

In its simplest form, VA support is "do work, record time, invoice time". The end. That is how many VAs work and certainly for ad-hoc projects where you don't need support every month, it's perfect. Just pay-as-you-go. For new clients, many VAs will insist on a deposit before starting work.

It will vary business to business, but VAs usually use a timesheet system that rounds up to the nearest five minutes. Some might be 15, others might be to the nearest second, everyone is slightly different.

If we are working on your stuff, emailing you about your stuff or sometimes even thinking about your stuff, we are on the clock. I say thinking about because it is our brains that you are paying for. If I have to sit and think for 90 seconds about how to solve a particular problem, if it's your problem, then it's on the clock. Unless it's 3am and just bugging me, that is free, but you can make a generous donation to my therapist if you feel it's appropriate.

Normally you can see your timesheet, either at month end or live if you are that interested in the detail of the time spent. For some of our larger clients we split our timesheets into the different people we support, so you get some really good data on how much support people are using and whether that's a bit too much or they should be using more. Sometimes VAs might relax the obsessive recording and give you a fixed monthly price once they have a sense of how many hours you use. Some months you may use a little more, some a little less but they figure it balances in the end.

Some clients even use our time recording to bill time back to their client if we are part of the contract with that client. Where the end client doesn't have any project support, for example, my client might suggest they can provide it via us and our hours for that project are billed on. We have several projects where our costs are covered by the end client and are factored into our clients' proposals.

If you are likely to need continuous support and want your VA to save time for you every week then you may well be asked to buy a retainer package of hours. Some VAs will only work in retained hours as it really helps with planning. Occasionally VAs offer a discount for retained hours, but not always. Retained hours are almost always paid for upfront. Contracts will differ, but often hours that go over a retained amount are charged at a non-retained rate.

In terms of managing the hours on a retainer, some VAs will flag up if you are near the end of your hours, some will send you weekly updates, and some will give you a link so you can check. There may or may not be an option to roll unused hours into the following month, it will depend on your contract.

Having a VA hold time for you is really helpful. You know that they have allocated time in the month to do your work, a guarantee you don't necessarily get with ad-hoc hours as they may be too busy to pick up the task. But it's important to note that having a VA on a retainer still does not give you access to them fulltime; they will still be working with multiple clients.

Having the fixed budget for the retainer is helpful for most businesses too. You know what your outlay will be and unless you're asking your VA for a lot more work than estimated, you will be able to plan your spend. It's also an encouragement to make you think of tasks to give to your VA. If those hours are sat there unused, it focuses your mind on what you could hand over.

There are also negatives to booking retained hours. Firstly, it can be really tricky until you get started to know how many hours you'll need to get the work done. Often for the first few months it's a bit of a finger-in-the-air guesstimate. If we aren't clear with a new client what the volume of work is, we often start with ad hoc until we see a pattern and then we move over to retained if it is more cost effective.

The other downside of a retainer is that if you don't use your hours, you will probably lose them. Your VA will likely be chasing you for work if you haven't sent any over, but there is a risk that if you retained twenty hours for the month but ignored your VA for three weeks, they aren't going to be able to use twenty hours in one week! So, if you are thinking retained hours is the way forward, it's going to work much better for all concerned if you have a steady flow of work rather than sporadic bursts of activity.

If you want a heads up if you have used more than 50% (or 75%, or whatever) of your retained hours mid-month, tell your VA so they can flag it. Some people use their retained hours and then pause on any work until the start of the next month. Most VAs will work with you to ensure you aren't spending more than you think. Our timesheets are fairly sophisticated, so we are able to do that easily.

Many people prefer to use ad hoc hours. Even when they are using more than enough for a retainer, they prefer not to be constrained by a number. Assuming your VA is happy to work with this then the benefit is that you can use as much or as little time as you like. There's an obvious benefit to this: if you don't have much work one month it won't cost you as much. However, there are a few things to be aware of before you decide this is the route you want.

Many VAs hold retained time and only do ad hoc work around this. If you aren't a regular retained client, you might ask them to do something and they may not have capacity, so you'll have to wait. Which might be fine if you are a planner or can see work coming ahead of time but might not work for you if you need a quick turnaround.

Tiny bits of client work are not ideal for VAs. Anyone who has done project work knows that small projects take more time than they really should. And this is the case for very small bits of VA work. If you are a client that doesn't generate much work, you will sadly be further down the priority list than someone using two hours a day. However, even with limited work coming in you will likely be taking up headspace for your VA, they will need to check your email and or task list or Slack even if there is nothing to see and this can be annoying. Some VAs may not even take you on or might fire you pronto if you aren't giving them a sensible amount of work. Of the VAs that I surveyed, more than 25% had fired a client because the work wasn't enough or was too "bitty".

This isn't us just being difficult. Without a certain amount of work, we can't get to understand you and your business. And therefore, we can't make an impact. When we're only doing random tasks without any depth or ongoing involvement in the business it's hard to get under the skin of what support you need and therefore make suggestions to take more on. It becomes a vicious circle: we don't have enough work, we can't see the bigger picture, we can't see opportunities for more work, we don't get any more work.

It can feel rather futile and frustrating, and you may well find yourself given the old heave-ho to make way for a client that is going to grow into something more fulfilling. We're running businesses and therefore will make business decisions about certain types and amounts of work.

When you don't give a VA enough work, you won't feel the benefit of them. If you're only interacting with your VA to give them one task at a time and there's nothing continuous for them to do between times and take off your load, it won't feel like a valuable resource.

I've had many people come to me having previously had a VA and said, "oh it didn't really work" and I'd be willing to guess this is because they don't really have enough work for a VA to do so it was bitty, frustrating and a waste of time. Or the communication wasn't up to scratch. Just because your list of ten tasks feels long to you, doesn't make it enough of a role for a VA. That's why in this book we're looking at your day-to-day tasks, everything that currently makes up your role, not just the work that's a bit annoying.

Personal versus Business

If you've ever worked with a PA before, did they do "work work" or personal work? Or a bit of both? Many VAs won't do purely personal work. We don't at Personally Virtual, despite our name. We support mostly business-to-business firms rather than individuals. Or if we're supporting an individual, it's in their business, not in their life.

There are Personal VAs that will support families and people that need help with their non-work lives. Booking holidays, sorting car insurance, managing multiple properties, even finding dog walkers and queuing for passports. But by and large, these VAs specialise in that kind of work. That doesn't mean that your business VA won't sort out some flowers or a gift or even get you a car to the airport for your holiday, but if you look down the list of things that you need doing and the majority of it is life admin, then you need to make sure when you look for a VA that they're happy doing that kind of work. Not all are - personally, I can't bear my own life admin, let alone someone else's! It's easy without an understanding of the industry to think all tasks are equal, but that isn't the case. Not that there's a hierarchy, but the kind of VA you need to work in your business, talk to your prospects and manage your new CRM project is unlikely to get much of a kick out of ordering school uniforms and sitting on hold to British Gas for you.

There are both PAs and VAs that specialise in personal management, household management, that type of thing. In years gone by this kind of service was really only for the uber rich High Net Worth folk who need oysters from Loch Fyne shipping to their yacht in Cannes or want to delegate hiring nannies and chefs to someone else.

With the advent of VAs, having a private VA is now an option for the more regular amongst us who are just overwhelmed by the sheer amount of stuff it takes to get through life. If you have a high stress busy job, adding the admin of a house and possibly several children on to that is an awful lot. You can have a cleaner and a nanny, but it's still on someone's mental load to ensure that they are booked at the right time, informed about holidays, paid correctly and so on. A personal VA can absolutely be a solution for a busy household if that's what you need. Just be clear from the outset that it's personal tasks that will take up the volume of time, so you get the right person to support you.

Contracts, data, tax law and security

I'm going to summarise this briefly here because we touch on these considerations more in Chapter Six on the hiring process. The bonus chapter at the end of the book also contains a deep dive into these subjects with Annabel Kaye, a legal specialist in these areas, so turn there to get your technical questions answered.

A properly set up VA will be managing their data and client data in a professional way according to where they're based and where their clients are based. Their business will have a data policy, as they will be storing data about their clients.

They'll have dedicated and appropriate IT kit and quite possibly support for that kit, or a backup machine in case of an IT crisis. At Personally Virtual we are Cyber Essentials Accredited, which means that all the team must hit a set of criteria on their IT kit and setup to ensure we're keeping as safe as possible.

Experienced VAs will only work with clients once a contract is in place. A contract isn't essential (although absolutely recommended) but a data processing agreement should be in place before any work begins so your VA knows how you want data to be handled and stored. This can form a part of the contract or might be a separate document. There should be clauses on confidentiality or a separate NDA. As another business, a VA owns the copyright to any work they do unless they have a clause in their contract that changes this.

Taking on a self-employed VA, you need to be careful that you don't start treating them like an employee. Your relationship with your VA should be business-to-business. There are various tests that split people into Workers and Self-employed. For example, do they have control of when and how they do the work? Are you expecting them to work regular hours? If you treat your VA as a worker and are audited by HMRC (His Majesty's Revenue and Customs), you're likely to be liable for their taxes. Thus, you need to make sure their contract is clear and that you're working to that contract in your day-to-day dealings with your VA. In particular, be happy for them to send a substitute to cover their work.

Associates

An associate is essentially a subcontractor to a Lead VA. The Lead VA will find the work and contract with the client and the associate will do the work.

Associate VAs are all running their own businesses, alongside being an associate. They're just as qualified and skilled as other VAs. In my case I believe that most of my team are more skilled diary managers than I am, and I'm absolutely fine with that!

Every Lead VA will work slightly differently with their associates. There are some that work a bit like an accountancy, where you email your accountant, and they email you back your accounts, but you know that they had one of the team do the work. You just never really see that person. Your contact is with your accountant only. In this case, the lead VA will pass on tasks and get them back and send them on. My business works very differently; my team work closely with the end client and build a relationship. That's vital to how we work and crucial in delivering an amazing service, so I don't get in the way of that.

Some VAs are both associates **and** use associates themselves! I did this for a long time. Being an associate potentially gives a VA access to jobs that they wouldn't be able to get on their own. Associates earn less money by going through a Lead VA than by working directly with a client, as the Lead VA or agency takes a cut. As such, the work must be worth it, either in volume, or interest or people. Being a VA is incredibly flexible and we can choose who we want to work with. That decision can be based on any number of reasons – we like the client, we like the internal team, the work is interesting, the money is good. It's not always about the money - I stuck with an associate job for years after it was not the best financial decision to keep going with it, simply because I loved the people I worked with.

Sometimes it can feel a bit weird when you are recommended to a VA and they say, "that will be my associate Julia who is best placed to help you". If it was a personal introduction, you may have wanted to work with the lead VA and anyone else feels like a bit of a downgrade. That's not the case. Lead VAs only introduce associates to a client or a prospect if they really think it's the best solution. And chances are, their other option is just saying no, and you'll need to go on a hunt for someone else anyway. As I've said, most of my team have better diary management skills than me. I'm not terrible by any means, but they are top-of-their-game-amazing and I'm, you know, good. It's our reputation on the line when we subcontract in an associate so we will have done our due diligence on them and you know that we've checked their insurance, their references and their set up.

So, if someone says to you, "I'm at capacity, but would you like to meet my associate?" you have nothing to lose and everything to gain by taking the meeting. After all, would you rather work with someone who has the capacity and skills to do the job as handpicked by a peer, or be looked after by an over-stretched and harried VA who has overloaded themselves?

As we discussed in Chapter Three, your contract with your VA should allow them to send you a substitute or sub, i.e., an associate if they choose to do so. I know it sounds quite scary having someone else work in place of your VA, but it really doesn't need to be. You'll need to ensure the tech works if your VA sends a sub and they'll make sure you are fully in the loop. Your VA won't bring in anyone they don't absolutely believe can do the job. This is their reputation and their relationship with you on the line, they are unlikely to risk that by bringing in someone hopeless. Your VA gets a much-needed holiday and doesn't come back to a mountain of work, and you get continued support. Trust your VA to make it work for you.

The other huge benefit of using a VA with an associate model is that if you need a specific skill set and the Lead VA doesn't have it, they can put in an associate that does. I have a little black book of potential associates that are my "normal" types of associates, diary ninjas, ex EA, super organised and super smart. But I also have a list of VAs for when I need something specific. Really complex board meetings or shareholder work? I know just the person. Internal systems a total mess and need processes putting in? I have just the one. Multiple languages needed? Yep. GDPR expertise? Yes. And sometimes on a job you need to bring in an expert for a specific project or a short period of time. The use of associates makes that really easy for the client as we can pull in someone with expertise in a particular area without a lot of fuss.

Working Onsite

You'd be amazed how many people ask if we can "pop into the office". The clue is in the name "virtual". In Chapter three we looked at whether you need someone in person or if it might just be nice to have the option to see your VA in person on occasion.

Being virtual is what makes us efficient, according to the most recent SVA (Society of

Virtual Assistants) Virtual Assistant survey[4], 57% of VAs don't work onsite. Those that do, usually charge extra for this.

If you are ever likely to need someone on the ground, it's worth laying that out upfront when you recruit. I know VAs that have supported their clients at events, conferences, workshops and meetings in person and been happy to do so. Be aware that because we can't be on the clock for anyone else in that time (including travel time, most likely) we will be charging you. Some VAs charge a different rate for travel time, some charge a different rate for onsite work and some just won't do it at all, thank you no. Check with your VA when you contract with them if you are ever likely to ask them to do in-person work.

No one can see into the future so if in person things come up and we aren't local enough, or

---

[4] Source: UK Virtual Assistant Survey 2023 (SVA) - for more information please visit www.societyofvirtualassistants.co.uk

aren't able to support you at an event, most VAs have amazing networks and are problem solvers, so if you need someone in person for something, likely we can help you find someone.

I hope that in this chapter I've given you a good idea about how VAs interact with their clients. We are jugglers of clients, recorders of time as well as bringers of calm and efficiency!

In this next section we're going to look at how you and your new VA can set up a working partnership that will put Fred and Ginger to shame before we move into the practicalities of hiring your very own rock-star VA.

***

ACTION STEPS

1. Think about how you might work with a VA as a "second brain".

2. Are the hours a VA works important to you or not? It may well be that it doesn't matter at all what hours they work as long as deadlines are met.

3. Start considering your budget.

    a. Do you have enough work for a VA to take on?

    b. Think about whether you have a preference for an ad hoc or retained contract – there are benefits to both.

4. Do you mostly have business work that needs doing or is it personal?

Five

Ensuring a Great Working Partnership

Having the right assistant can make **you** amazing, which is why I want to make you and your VA the best partnership since Torville and Dean. I've been a PA and VA for over 20 years, and I've seen and been a part of some truly phenomenal supporting relationships. There's a secret tactic behind almost all of them: the client lays the groundwork for their new VA before the contract is even signed.

As well as choosing the right person or company, there's much you can do ahead of them starting to get you off on the right foot and help the VA become a positive force in your business as quickly as possible. This chapter will help you do exactly that.

The best VA relationship is one based on mutual respect for the other's strengths. You know what you are great at and what your brilliance is. You probably also know where you need to bring in someone else to buffer areas that aren't so great. Clearly you need to be looking for a VA that has the bits you are missing.

The first part of flourishing with that complementary VA is having a really granular understanding of how things work now. Until you get detailed on what you currently do, it will firstly, be tricky to explain to someone else and secondly, be harder to spot opportunities to outsource. So, pull out that task list you made in Chapter One and add anything you forgot the first time around.

The second part is a more holistic way of thinking about this VA relationship, which I've called unpacking your backpack. The rather brilliant Annabel Kaye (see the Bonus chapter) came up with this analogy and I like it, so I'm going to steal it. These are the ways of working that are not contractual enough to end up in anyone's Terms and Conditions but are nonetheless important to the quality of the relationship. Keeping them in mind during recruiting will help ensure that the VA you choose will be a good fit with you. I'll give you some real-life examples later in the chapter to get you thinking about your own backpack.

The Bible of You

Ahead of bringing a new person into your business, you need to understand how things work now in order to be able to explain it to them. Ideally, this should be written down in some shape or form. Where there are any processes that your new VA will touch on, even if they aren't directly actioning anything, they should know how they work in your business.

It's also worth thinking about your values and the business values as you create this. Your VA will need to know these to work to them. Even if they are a bit vague, get them out of your head and on to paper.

This doesn't need to be an epic tome, despite the title, but in a larger business it is likely to be more complex as you will need to give an overview of other departments and how they work where there is a connection point.

Your Bible will vary depending on what you want your VA to do and how you create it. It is totally up to you. One client we had downloaded his life into Trello cards. I did my invoicing process for my VA on PowerPoint with some flow charts.

For diary and travel management, if you have until now been doing this yourself you will have to really think about your preferences and make sure that what is in your head as automatic, moves to being visible for someone else. If you use a personal diary (especially if you use the one on your phone) you'll need to make sure that your VA has a way to access this or merge it. Ical / Apple phone calendars are a nightmare for VAs – they really do cause issues! This is firstly because it's really easy to accidentally add something to the wrong calendar which then won't show in your "normal" calendar. Secondly, some people in small businesses use Ical as their main and only calendar and it is not designed as a work calendar. It doesn't have the proper delegate functionality you get with Google or MS365 and is generally really glitchy for VAs to work with.

Business Processes

There are entire books written about mapping business processes, done thoroughly and properly and in big businesses it is extraordinarily complex. Happily, we don't need to do that, we simply need look at the processes you have and how they will impact your VA.

Where your VA will be picking up all or part of a process, they are clearly going to need a lot more detail. Some tasks and notes can be as simple as

- Weekly, check my inbox for receipts and forward them to Finance.

That's it. A weekly task to scan your inbox for any money spent and send the information on for processing elsewhere. If no other information is needed it can be that simple. If that receipt needed billing back to a client, or had to have a project code added, you'd obviously need to add in more steps on where to find that information so that the Finance team has everything they need to accurately do their next steps.

Other processes that may be good to map, even if only in a light way, are your sales process, your invoicing process, a standard project and so on. As you think through how these work for you, you may see ways your VA can expedite the flow.

Here's an example of a flow chart showing a basic sales process and areas where a VA can support it.

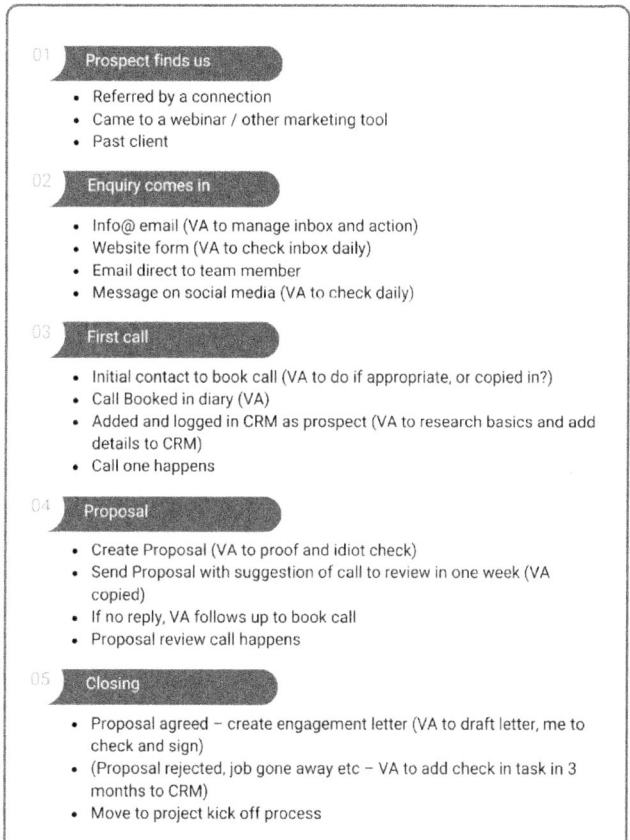

Example Sales Process

In this you can see parts of that process where I have decided that my VA can take some actions. They can also take some of the mental load with this as following-up type tasks are given to them, ensuring that keeping in touch with prospects and using the CRM properly is built into their workflow. Obviously, they would check in with you if anything got stuck. In this example the VA is client facing, they are emailing to book things in and check. You might decide that is too much too soon and add those bits in later if that feels more appropriate. I haven't put the VA down as creating the proposal, but if your business had a fairly standard set of things to sell, they certainly might be able to create a first draft from a template and leave you to pad out the specifics of this client.

I'm going to give you a few more examples just to get your brain juices flowing on how this might work. Clearly, your business is unique and none of these processes will match yours exactly, but I hope it gets you thinking about the types of tasks that a VA could pick up.

01 New clients

- On signed engagement letter, VA to check the invoicing process and complete any new supplier forms, chase any purchase orders etc
- VA to flag any issues with me ahead of month-end

02 Track work

- New multi-month jobs are added to the work spreadsheet detailing invoice amounts per month based on engagement letter payment schedule
- Any one-off jobs or sessions are added to the work spreadsheet

03 Double check

- Month end, we both go through the work spreadsheet and check it for any missing work or delayed starts
- Ensure any billable expenses are billed back (see expenses process)
- Add any new work starting next month.

04 Invoicing

- Invoices are created and sent in Xero (VA)

05 Chasing

- For new or tricky clients, VA sends an email to check that all has been safely received and if anything else is needed in order to pay the invoice on time
- Late payments chased after 1, 3 and 5 days overdue (VA) and flagged to me if later

06 Reconcile

- Payments in on Xero reconciled against invoices (VA)

Example Invoicing Process

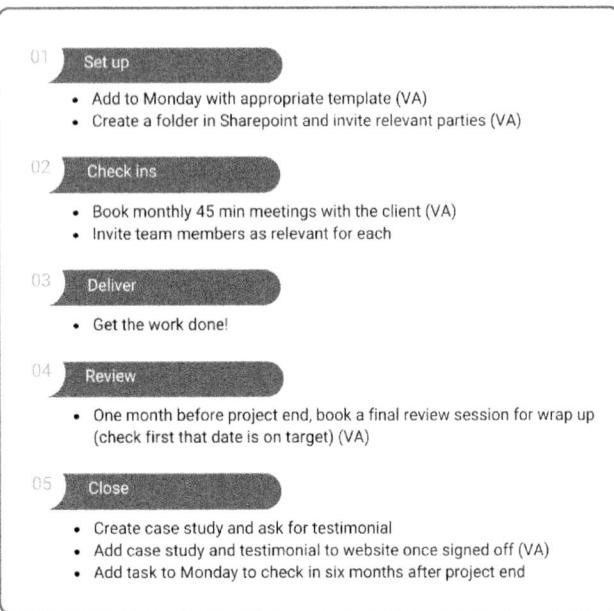

Example Project Process

Your brand

It's also helpful to remember that your VA will be a representative of your brand as they talk to other businesses. If there are things that you do that you want them to also do, you need to be clear about it. Think about your tone, your VA won't be talking to people (or more likely writing to people) in the exact same tone as you because you know them, however, it is really helpful for your VA to have some guidelines.

Think about your company brand, if you are Eejit Llama Industries, is it ok to shorten that to ELI or not? It's the same with any of your products or services they might be talking about. Some companies are very acronym-averse, others use so many you may need to create a dictionary for your VA so they know what the hell anything is.

Most people these days are slightly more informal in tone, but some industries still have a traditional slightly old-school vibe. Is it OK to email people with "Hi Ed" or with some people would you expect "Dear Dr Foster" from your assistant? Are there certain clients or cultures that you work with where a different etiquette is needed? What is your view on emojis internally and externally?

How about your personal brand? Do you have a particular title you prefer? If your VA is sending a bio to someone for publication, what job title do you use and how do you like your name written? Some people informally go by "Dan" but for events and more formal events are a "Daniel". Do you routinely use letters after your name to show your education, an MBE or similar? When would you do that and when would you not?

Your VA is going to be become a part of your brand and you need to ensure you help them reflect that accurately – in tone, in the email address and with the email signature they use and also in what they are saying. A good VA will soon learn your tone and start to build their own relationships with your main contacts, and then they will undoubtedly be a little more themselves. But with VIPs and new potential clients or political connections and so on, it's good to have a clear set of rules to work to as a starting point.

Unpacking your backpack – setting expectations

What are your day-to-day expectations for working with your new VA?

One way to think about this is, what might you find annoying if a VA did it?

If I do this exercise, I'd uncover a few things that I would find annoying in communications, for example, having conversations about the same thing in several places and my VA calling me at a non-booked time. I have a lot of team members that don't work school holidays so it would be unhelpful for me if my VA did that as well. And I use my VA to cover for my time off, so I need someone who works five days a week.

Annabel Kaye, author of the bonus chapter later, has an example that always sticks in my mind. This was a client who had a regular Zoom webinar on a Wednesday night at 6PM with a wide audience. Although the VA knew about this, it wasn't clear that there were any actions required of her for it; she wasn't helping host the Zoom or sending invites. As far as the VA was concerned there was no involvement for her in this event. However, this was the busiest time of the week for the client on email as people managed to lose the webinar link, or got locked out, or couldn't find the pre-work or whatever in the hours running up to the call. The VA picked her kids up from school on a Wednesday and Friday and took them to swimming lessons until about 18.00. The client had an expectation that the VA would be there on a Wednesday late afternoon, early evening but had at no point made that clear to the VA. Similarly, had the VA said upfront "I finish work at 15.00 on a Wednesday and Friday" this would have come to light sooner.

No one is at fault here, it's just that expectations aren't managed on either side.

What are your expectations? Are they reasonable? FYI being able to ring your VA at any time and expect them to pick up and deal with a task immediately is not reasonable.

Part of my backpack when I am talking to new clients is that I am not available on the phone all day every day. I tell my clients to email me or add a task to a task list (if we use one); the phone is only for our weekly catch ups or a crisis. And an actual time-sensitive crisis, not "I think I need to move that meeting next week because we're having a boiler fitted" – for that, email me! When we're working across multiple clients, we have to be able to fully focus on that client. You wouldn't like it if we were on the clock and billing you and got interrupted by a call and we lost our focus. We might stop the clock for the call, but it'll still take time for us to get back into the zone after an interruption. According to a study done by the University of California[5], it takes 23 minutes to get back into the zone after an interruption. Pre-scheduled calls or emergencies only, please.

If you like to download your brain by speaking, that's totally fine. I did this with a client. He'd record a voice memo and email it to me. I wasn't interrupted but he could quickly download his stream of consciousness. I'd then pick that up next time I was signed into his timesheet because I'd know it wasn't urgent. When my phone rings, I assume it's an urgent thing that needs me to action something ASAP so even if I don't answer it, it

---

[5] Gloria Mark, Daniela Gudith and Ulrich Klocke, The Cost of Interrupted Work: More Speed and Stress

will have caught my attention. The advantage of this for my clients is that because I know that they know to only call me in an emergency, I will always pick up the phone if they call because I know it's an emergency. It's the opposite of crying wolf. I believe you need me because you never call me and it's been eight months since you last did!

The expectations you have can be daft things that you may not have considered if you haven't worked with an assistant before. As an example, when you send someone a task, do you like an acknowledgment or are you happy to just let someone get on with it? At first you may need a quick "got it" response or a thumbs up or whatever it may be, so you know the message is received. As you build trust you may feel you don't need it anymore. Or that extra inbox traffic might be an irritation. I rather like that Microsoft has given us "reactions" now so a quick thumbs up can be added as an acknowledgement. Or they may be more values based. And your VA will have things as well. The more you think of them, the better.

I liken this stage of the process to a conversation I had with a new cleaner once. "Is there anything you don't do?" I said.

"No, I do everything" she replied. Marvellous.

And then she cleaned the house beautifully but didn't empty a single bin. When I asked her about it, she didn't think of bin-emptying as part of cleaning. I did think of bin-emptying as part of house cleaning. No one is right or wrong here, we just needed to have had a much more in-depth conversation upfront rather than us both working on (wrong) assumptions. Some cleaners won't empty bins, some won't open anything to clean inside it, other will but not ovens, some do windows, some don't. It is a minefield. And that's just cleaning! I now have a list of what I would like cleaned and how often so if I have to change cleaners, we can talk through it and flag upfront any issues. This is the way to think about your new VA relationship. Don't let there be any assumptions that are lingering unanswered.

Partnering on Managing a Diary

I am rather a geek when it comes to diary management and could cheerfully write a whole book on that topic. However, realising that not everyone gets a VA for diary management, I shall curb my enthusiasm to some extent.

There is a myth that diary management is easy and anyone can do it. If it's just lobbing a meeting into a gap, you are entirely right, AI can do that seamlessly already as can any number of meeting booking systems. However, what most people need more of in their working life is time, and diary management, done correctly, can help you maximise your time. That might be as practical as your VA ensuring that your days at home and out and about are sensible, so you aren't commuting in for just one meeting three days in a row, or they could be getting into some serious time strategy planning with you. When I take on a new diary job, I'll be asking a page full of questions, even down to, "do you work better early or late? When are you most able to do your best creative work?" because those times shouldn't be used up with easy meetings where possible.

Our team are diary ninjas – that is what they do and most have 15 years or more looking after the most complex diaries you've ever seen. Your average VA won't be working at that level but between you, you can create some parameters for your diary to carve out more time for what you should be focusing on. They can help you protect time for deep work and to prepare for meetings (it's much easier for someone that isn't you to do this!), they can prioritise and move things around to make room for that vital prospect or client call. And they can sense check requests from people for your time to make sure that you aren't spread too thin unnecessarily. Does that meeting really need to be an hour or could the same be accomplished in 40 minutes? "Could it push into next week?" They can ask those questions where for the sake of speed you'd just put in whatever was requested without perhaps looking at the bigger picture.

If you recall the section on your brilliance, you'll remember that it's quite a mental feat to wedge that into small amounts of time. With your VA's help, you can perhaps try and have a day or two a week with no meetings so you can get some time to focus on your brilliance without interruptions.

I'd suggest that during your onboarding you really think about what your ideal working week would look like. Not that it's realistic to think it'll ever happen! But if you know what perfection is, your VA can help you work towards that.

There will be some diary "rules" that you and your VA will agree on – that might be "no meetings on a Friday", or "work at home every Monday" as a big picture item. There will also be nuances – how fast do you want to get a new prospect call in and what will you bump to make that work? Are there any meetings that you really shouldn't need to get involved in that we should delegate elsewhere? Are there meeting types that need preparation time or others invited as standard? Do you have board meetings that need formal agendas issuing or packs preparing? Do you have a limit on how many early starts or late finishes you do? Maybe you find particular types of meetings quite draining and need to cap their number in a day, or a week and perhaps allow buffers.

Your VA can help you keep on top of meeting preparation, keep track of agenda items and, if you prefer, can make sure that every meeting that goes in has an agenda or a topic, so you know what to plan for. You can also have your VA confirm meetings ahead of time. I am quite anti-meeting confirming as on occasion it seems to remind people that it's there and gives them the opportunity to say "oh, actually no, something has come up, can we reschedule?" which they probably would have been too embarrassed to do on the day. But that may be a small price to pay to avoid no shows!

Your VA can also start and manage a list of preferred venues and hotels for you, for different events and different people. You will likely have some already but as we research venues in new areas, new overseas places that are added to your regular work life, this can build up.

Our team have an in-depth sheet to fill out with a huge amount of questions because we focus really heavily on complex diary management. Other roles may not need this. My suggestions on the basics of what you might need to consider, depending on the complexity of your life are below.

- What are your non-negotiables around working hours, e.g. school pick-ups, number of evenings or early starts, days you must be at home / in the office / with clients.
- Do you have a standard length of meeting? What should be in person versus virtual. And if virtual, what is your preferred system?
- What gaps, if any, do you need between meetings?
- Do you need chunks of time protected to work quietly?
- How long does it take you to get to the office and what is the earliest start you would go in for / latest you'd stay for?
- Your preferred venues for meetings, coffees, meals, events.
- You key clients and contacts that should be prioritised for meetings as well as any regular internal meetings or networking meetings your VA should know about and understand.

- What unwritten rules are there with your diary? Think about what would horrify you if it went in if you want to think about your innate boundaries!

Travel Planning

Having your VA plan travel is a huge time-saver, particularly for complex trips. These are things that they will need to know.

- Which is your nearest station, and do you prefer tickets booked? If so any preferences on seating or standard versus first class tickets?
- Which is your nearest airport, and do you tend to drive there or get a cab or public transport?
- Who do you book flights with? Is there a company travel agent or is it done ad hoc direct via the provider or a search on rates?
- Do you want your flights and trains to be fully refundable and flexible or would you rather get a cheaper but less flexible option?
- Are any company or client budgets in place or is it on a case-by-case basis?

- Do you have any preferences on economy flights, Premium Economy or Business, or does it depend on the client or length of journey?
- Do you have any loyalty cards for airlines or hotel chains you want to use when booking?
- Do you have any hotel preferences, e.g. walkable into town, with a gym or pool, specific star ratings? Do you ever book AirBnBs or similar as an alternative? Are there any hotels where your clients have a preferred rate?

Inbox management

Handing over your inbox to a VA requires a good deal of trust and it may not be something that you feel comfortable with immediately. Access doesn't necessarily mean that they are doing anything in there - you may give your VA access simply so they can log in and check things if they need the background on a meeting, or so they can track down receipts as part of a bookkeeping task. However, you may want their help in managing emails or even actioning and responding to emails.

If you decide that you want help managing your inbox, you will need to create a series of guidelines for your VA to follow, whether that is deleting any spam or filing everything that is read after one week or whatever it may be. It's very possible that your new VA will have suggestions on how to manage your inbox and an awful lot more questions once they've had a look at how you run your inbox. But it is worth thinking ahead about how you work with your inbox now and what is realistically possible. And again, what would horrify you if it happened to your inbox? What will horrify you versus me would be very different because email is a tool we all use differently. Think about how you use it – does it become a task system for you or is it purely communication? Do you move information out of email to another place, like a CRM or your diary or a task list or is stored email vital for information retrieval in the future? Are you CC'ed on a lot that you need to just be aware of rather than action or does everything in your inbox represent something you need to do? All these things will influence how you manage your inbox and how your VA can help you. You don't need to do anything at this point, just give it some thought for a few minutes ahead of talking to your VA. They'll ask the questions, but it is helpful to have given the answers some consideration ahead of time.

You can also get your VA to reply to people on your behalf. This is not as terrifying as it sounds! You can tell them what the answer is, in quick form, and they can write a nice reply. You can download the actual answers to emails with whatever communication system you have agreed ("yes to joining that conference, can you politely say no to Jen, it's too soon, we'll be in touch and then the Robert email, I'm happy to meet but not urgent, thanks" you can even do that on a voice memo for speed and then email it) and then the VA will craft a nice email on your behalf, quite possibly copying themselves in to pick up further actions. When you first start doing this you might want your VA to craft the emails and leave them in your Drafts so you can quickly review and send. I realise that this sounds more time consuming than replying yourself, but it's building knowledge and expertise for your VA to be able to take more on in time.

You'll soon get into a rhythm and in time your VA can take the lead and the process is more "re todays emails, I'm going to do a nice no to that charity (we support

Save the Children etc), I'll reply and book Adrian, Sue and James but push Justin out until after your trip. Do you want to reply to the new prospect, or shall I draft something for you to check and send, I thought copy in Priya so she can attend the meeting as well?".

I supported a CEO for many years and by the time she moved on, I could write an email on her behalf and a few weeks later neither she or I could tell which of us wrote it – I had her style and tone down to a tee.

If you want your VA to reply as you from your inbox, or if there are standard responses to things, it can be useful to have some template emails using your language. Eventually they will create more or some shortcuts, but having some upfront will be a good start. What are you asked most often? Do you have a stock response for things like a new prospect, someone wanting you to come and speak at an event, a journalist requesting an interview, someone wanting to pick your brains about what it is you do, someone wanting a job, a charity after a donation and so on. Think of the kinds of emails that come in, to you or a shared inbox, and create some typical replies. There will be nuances of course, but if you have a set of rules, it becomes easier to power through your inbox without constantly asking questions. It may be as simple as "thanks so much for getting in touch about a role. I've copied in Jayde in HR who will be in touch about how to apply formally". And that's the rule for job hunters. If there are other people who pick these things up, that's the standard, your VA just needs to know what goes to who.

The two of you should decide on a system so that you always know what is where in your inbox. I love categories and had one that was "Kathy replied" and one that was "Kathy sorting" so that when my client saw that he knew he could ignore it or check in with me if he wanted a status update. I'd usually then file them away after 48 hours so they weren't cluttering the inbox. But I wanted to be sure he'd seen them and knew I was on the case.

I hope that this section has given you some food for thought ahead of the next stage, which is (squeal!) finding and hiring your new VA.

***

ACTION STEPS

1. Write the Bible of You—how does everything work in your business? Go task by task, process by process, for anything your VA will touch.

2. Unpack your backpack—what are the qualitative, relational, and time-based expectations you have for your VA? What would annoy you if they did or didn't do it?

Six

Let's do this! Finding and Hiring your New VA

This section is quite deliberately towards the end of the book. With the information you've read and the action steps you've taken so far, you should know what kind of work you want a VA to take on and have some clear thoughts on what that working relationship might look like.

I'm going to take you through that process from start to finish to ensure you have the best possible chance of getting the right VA first time.

How do you see your VA relationship working?

This may sound like a stupid question, but it is really key. The kind of help you're actually looking for will change how much energy you invest in the search. Do you just want to have available to you, on a really informal ad hoc basis, one VA, or maybe a few different folks, who you can send specific tasks to when they come up? If that's the case, as long as they have the skills and are professionally set up, that should be enough. That is what you are looking for.

Don't bother with a long process to look for someone to pick up a couple of hours of work. It's low risk if it doesn't work out. Find someone fast via recommendation, have a quick chat and then get going. You'll still need a contract and it's worth doing some due diligence if they have any kind of access to your data but really you want to keep this a simple transaction. No one wants to spend two hours for free talking about and organising a one-hour job. Just get on with it.

Are you instead looking for a VA who will work alongside you for the foreseeable future, or someone to do a specific but full project with an end goal? For an ongoing relationship, you need to dig a little deeper into working styles and preferences to really get a great thing going. That is going to take more effort and more time but it's worth investing to get the right fit. And, as we saw in the last chapter, a large part of that is some self-examination—because unless you know how you prefer to work, you won't know what to ask for.

Some of these you'll ask whoever supports you to do, but other traits may well impact who you chose to work with. For example, some people are detailed folk. They want to know every stage of every task and have granular lists of where things are up to. Every email will be in full sentences, and they will probably be long and very thorough. Some VAs, myself included, find that way of working quite taxing. That's not to say we can't do it, an experienced VA will have worked with all sorts of people and have had to mould their working style accordingly, but it isn't our favourite way of working. It is extra effort as it doesn't come naturally. That kind of person would be much better matched with a VA who has a similar working style and is comfortable dealing in the details and sharing very frequently. They would find my natural tendency of replying to their carefully crafted 500-word email with "great, thanks" deeply frustrating!

Is having some fun at work important to you? For some people working with an outgoing, bubbly personality is a joy, for others who are more contained, a loud, bouncy, and vivacious character might be wearisome. However, two very strong personalities with huge amounts of drive might mean that you are missing between you, a more thoughtful and reflective element as you both go, go, go. Or it might push you both to amazing results.

Are there things you lack? I know several people who are a little brusque in their dealings with others, not because they aren't wonderful humans but because they are busy and get to the point. Both have VAs that write beautifully, in full, and with plenty of softness to counterbalance their slightly abrupt tone. If you aren't great at spelling, make sure your VA is excellent so they can proofread for you. You get the idea.

Do you need someone who is client facing? I have been on many client and prospects calls with clients and even done in-person workshops with clients. Clearly, they need to know that I'm going to represent them in a way that reflects their brand appropriately. In written communication my English and spelling needs to be good and in person I need to look and sound at least vaguely competent! They will also need to be in an appropriate time zone if you want them to be available for these types of things. If you would like them to attend the odd thing in person then again, they'll need to be based somewhere that is easily accessible.

Creating a detailed role spec

Whilst you aren't employing someone, you're contracting with another business, the hiring process will go more smoothly for everyone involved if you have a decent description of what you are looking for. It's called a role spec. That can take any form you like, but ideally it needs to list the tasks you want to get done, the kind of relationship you expect (ad hoc, ongoing), and a guess at how many hours you need.

The hours bit can be tricky. As a rule, people overestimate how many hours they need because they are coming from an employee mindset, so they think they need someone "part time, five mornings a week or equivalent". That's rarely the case. There's also a tendency when you're doing everything yourself to think things take hours. And for you, likely they do, as you're interrupted by your day job. But someone with dedicated time to spend can whip through things faster. So the best thing to do in your role spec is give a vague amount ("20-30 hours a month TBC" or whatever) and discuss it with the VAs you speak to about the work. They will have an idea of the hours you'll really require once you have a conversation about you and your business and what support you need.

Example of a really good role spec.

 ROLE SPEC

The business and people, an overview:

I'm Dave and I started Dave's Coaching in 2015. As well as taking on clients face to face, I also see clients on Zoom, and I have several online courses that people can purchase. I work with two associate coaches. Occasionally the three of us run team sessions together but most of the time we all work individually across our client base.

The business has got bigger and more complex in the last two years, and I need someone to work with me and take some of the load.

We're passionate about helping people be confident in their role and interactions with other people and we love what we do!

The role, an overview:

I would like to find a VA that can work alongside me and take on more as the role expands. The obvious day-to-day tasks are managing my diary, particularly client bookings, and sorting out travel where needed.

In addition, some clients have specific admin around online timesheets and portals, so I'd value some help with those. I'd also like you to send invoices and chase up late payers (we don't have many, just some can get stuck in big company bureaucracy).

This is a self-employed virtual role, and our initial estimate is that it will take around five hours a week, but we'd like someone who has flexibility if this varies a bit week to week.

ROLE SPEC

Tasks:
- Calendar management (Google) and sending invites to clients.
- Sending out pre-work as needed for any sessions.
- Making sure any workshops or sessions are held in appropriate spaces (liaison with client PA and/or booking external rooms at Regus or similar).
- Sending invoices monthly or at the end of a project.
- Following up with late payers.
- Monthly proofreading and sending out the Mailchimp newsletter.
- Maintaining the newsletter list.
- Occasional posts to LinkedIn.
- Tidying up PowerPoint presentations.
- Occasional blogs to upload to the website (WordPress).
- In time, other things that you think of that you can help me with!

About you:
- Excellent interpersonal skills and able to build relationships with clients and their PAs remotely and be happy to pick up the phone and speak to people if that's a better option.
- Reliable, do what you say you'll do, in a timely way.
- Attention to detail, great spelling and grammar.
- A positive and proactive attitude.
- Warm and friendly, can-do.

Skills needed:
- Great diary management skills using Google Cal, confident with multiple time-zones.
- Accurate administration for client portals (I'll show you how to use them).
- Good at researching cost-effective travel options.
- Mailchimp (intermediate).
- Wordpress (basic).
- Xero (basic).

Must haves:
- Proper self-employed set up.
- Appropriate IT kit that is kept up to date and has business level software.
- Insurance, professional indemnity to £500K or equivalent.
- If needed, AML registration and ICO registration.

This is a long spec, and you wouldn't use this as an advert but perhaps send it to interested parties.

Remember that you aren't hiring an employee, you are looking for a service to support you, so you won't be advertising an hourly rate. You'll want people to quote their rates, instead. Having said that, you should have in mind a budget.

The AML (anti-money laundering) registration is only relevant because there are accounts admin and Xero access tasks on the role spec. And not everyone would need it – those based overseas don't and there is a bit of a buffer for UK VAs under a threshold. However, it's there because if your UK VA applicants don't know what AML is, that should possibly wave some red flags. I'd argue that all UK VAs need to be registered with the ICO (Information Commissioners Office) but again, some may have done the tests to see if they should be and discovered they don't. Just make sure they know what it is and can explain why they do or don't have it.

The insurance amount listed here isn't a prescription. It may not matter to you if they only have £250K of insurance. But again, if they turn round and look blankly at you because they have none, it's a warning sign that they don't have their business set up properly.

Anyone taking their business seriously has these things in place. As well as having them on the spec, it's worth asking again when you meet them.

Creating your advert

When you are looking for your VA, you need a trimmed down version of the above. One possible summary of the above example is:

Looking for a professional and experienced VA to support our coaching business with diary management, travel, invoicing, Mailchimp and other admin. Estimate 20 hours per month but happy to discuss. This is a self-employed role, and you must be fully set up with insurance, ICO registration etc. If you want more information, please email dave@davescoaching.com

And then follow the process later in the chapter.

I would be cautious about where you put this ad though, you don't need hundreds of applications. We'll look later in the chapter at the best way to cast your net out to find your new VA.

Which Assistant?

Here we are going to look at some of the different kinds of VAs out there and the pros and cons of each so you can both understand the businesses of the folks you talk with and get a sense of which type of VA you might like to aim for.

The Freelance VA

The majority of VAs work as freelancers. It's just them and you contract with them directly. Typically, they would send you their terms and conditions and they'd explain how they work to you – their working hours, what they do about holidays and their specialist skills.

These VAs will almost certainly have multiple clients. They may also work as associates for other VAs or have associates work for them. At a certain point, that might become an agency, where a lead VA does most of the marketing and sales and they subcontract out most, if not all, of the work. There is a lot of overlap between freelancers and agencies. Most, but not all, agencies are a group of freelancers. Some agencies might employ their VAs but that won't change how they contract with you.

The benefit of having a freelance VA is that you are buying a service. Often, they have flexible contracts, and you can use them as much or as little as you want. Some work on retainer, as discussed in Chapter 3. Others may have minimum hour requirements, or you may have to pre-pay for hours in advance. But these are all things you can discuss when you meet them.

Agencies

There are various types of VA agency. Not all agencies are the same so it's worth checking when you're talking to them how they are set up and how they will resource your work. There are some (mostly the really large agencies) where you don't necessarily get a named VA, you send in tasks and whoever is free takes it on. That may well work for you if your need for a fast turnaround outweighs your need to have one stable person that you get to know and build a relationship with. It can also be great if you have lots of small projects that just need doing and sending back – tasks like audio typing, formatting documents and research. Standalone tasks like these are easy for VAs to pick up and complete without a huge amount of input or access to your systems.

If you want to have a more personal relationship with one VA then check that is how your selected agency works. In most cases, you will contract to the agency, or the Lead VA, and they will decide on the right resource from their stable of VAs, which may be one or more depending on the role or roles needing support. You may or may not get the opportunity to meet several of the team and pick the one you think is the best fit. That VA will then be your main day-to-day contact.

The benefit of using an agency is that you have a little bit of a buffer between you and the VA should anything not be working smoothly. You'll know (or absolutely check!) that the Lead VA has all the right contracts, insurance and data processing procedures in place to keep you safe.

Many agencies will offer holiday cover if your VA goes away or is off sick, so you won't be left high and dry. If you are having problems with your VA, having someone else to feedback to is helpful – they can suggest ways for you and your VA to work better together and if your VA isn't the right fit, they should be able to swap them for another member of the team. This gives you another layer of safety.

Online work sites

Sites like Fiverr and Upwork have become increasingly popular in recent years, especially for those on a budget. I don't know a single good VA who uses them – they have more than enough work through referrals, some of their own marketing and repeat business.

You may well get a bargain basement VA from one of these sites, but I strongly suspect that it won't be the quality kind of VA support that we're talking about in this book. I'm sure that there are amazing VAs on these sites. But finding them? It's really a race to the bottom of the price pile when you are looking for something as wide as VA support. That isn't an ideal way to find someone to have a business relationship with. Maybe it's ok for one task, a one off. But finding someone to do that one off probably takes longer than doing it yourself!

My advice? Leave these sites well alone.

Working with a friend or acquaintance

Say one of the school mums who used to do a bit of admin says she's happy to do some odds and ends for you. Before leaping at the opportunity, you must consider two things.

Number one, do they have a proper set up? Chances are, unless they are already a VA they don't. That leaves you—and potentially them—at risk in any number of ways.

Indulge me a moment in a little story.

I have two extremely furry border collies. I spend an insane amount of time grooming them. I have some brushes, scissors, and comb. All bought from Pets at Home ten years ago.

My friend says "you know your way around a fluffy tail, can you groom my dog? I'll bung you £20?" so I do. It's all great. Her dog looks fabulous, and I have £20 for a nice bottle of something.

Then she says "I'll share your details on Facebook. I bet loads of people in my dog group would like a groomer". She duly does this, I get some calls, some more bookings and before you know it, I'm £200 richer, cash in hand, thank you very much indeed.

The calls keep coming. I am wildly cheaper than any other the other local established groomers because they pay for training, proper equipment, insurance, and contracts and I have none of these things.

Then one day, I accidently slice a bit of dog leg with my not-very-sharp-scissors. There's blood. There's crying; me and the dog. I don't know canine first aid, so my living room is looking like a scene from psycho in about a minute and a half as I fail to stop the bleeding. There's a vet trip. It's expensive. The client expects my insurance to pay except that I don't have any. They are livid. The dog is a mess. The vet is also livid at my shoddy ways and wants to report me nine-ways to Sunday to anyone that will listen. And quite possibly HMRC are on that list.

Do you see where I'm going with this?

Obviously, I have never groomed anyone else's dog— this is made up. But you must factor in risk when you work with someone who isn't properly set up. Instead of blunt scissors, maybe they have a laptop from 2015 with no anti-virus and they send you an infected file. Perhaps they are helping you with some bookkeeping and they should be registered for anti-money laundering, and they aren't – at which point they are risking a huge fine. Maybe they won't be fully competent on all the software you use, and they mistakenly delete a key file.

It's tempting to think "oh it's just a bit of admin, what harm can it do" but it's your business, your hard-won clients, your data and your intellectual property that you're risking if you get the dog groomer mate without doing the proper checks.

Number two, what happens if something goes wrong? That's not to say something will go wrong, I know many friends that work together and it's brilliant. But it is worth having the conversation upfront with each other to try and protect your friendship if the work side of things doesn't go as planned.

Draw up some guidelines for yourselves. I know two friends that work together, and they have two different WhatsApp conversations so one is work and one is personal. That way they remind themselves of the boundaries. Be clear about having review meetings. Two friends I know set up a business and they have what they call "marriage guidance counselling" once a quarter with a coach just to check that everyone is on the same page.

Side-hustlers

There are two different types of people that are a VA outside of their main job.

The first kind is quite likely in a transition period. They are working part-time or fulltime just until they build up their client base enough that they can ditch the day job and be a fulltime freelancer. Many VAs start this way. This kind of person might work well for you if you don't need to be able to catch up with your VA through the day and they are happy to do a call if needed in the evenings. But if you want diary management and want others to be able to get hold of your VA in working hours, this might be frustrating unless they are in a different time zone—for example, if you are in the USA, an evening UK VA would be a good bet.

The second kind is a true side-hustler; they're a VA part time, their hours will be limited, and they may or may not being doing it long-term. (Have I mentioned how much I loathe the expression "side-hustle"? It makes my teeth itch. It just sounds somehow dodgy to me, like it's a con.) With the first kind of VA there is at least a future where they will have more hours free – you increasing your hours might even be enough for them to move to fully freelance. But with someone who only wants to do VA work in the margins this isn't likely to happen. My other concerns with a side-hustle VA who has no intention of making it a profession would be:

- Are they as committed as someone who is a career VA and does it day in and day out?

- Will they save up enough money for whatever it is they are working towards and then decide to stop?

- What happens if their day job gets busy or there is a crisis? They aren't playing with many spare hours if something elsewhere goes awry.

- Are they set up properly? Many don't realise that it doesn't matter if you bill five hours a week or 30, you still need the exact same set up in terms of proper equipment, insurance, ICO registration etc. That ends up being expensive if you are not doing many hours, so some of the more unscrupulous or unaware out there skip it thinking "it's just a bit of admin".

New VAs

We've all been new to something in our lives, and I certainly wouldn't say "don't ever work with a brand-new VA". I have VAs on my team that are new to being a VA. However, they are hugely experienced as an EA, usually twenty-plus years. The VA-specific elements, like using timesheets and invoicing, are things that as a Lead VA I can help them with. To me, it depends if they can do the work that is needed. That's why working through an agency can be really helpful as they get support on the bits that don't affect the end client.

There are a lot of brand-new VAs out there and some of them will be great because their previous work experience is amazing. The only difference is that they're working as freelancer not as an employed PA. But if they don't know the first thing about being a VA, you are back to the same issues as using a friend – they may not be properly set up and then that puts your business at risk. Of course, having read this book you now know about the kind of things that they should have as part of a proper business set up so you can send them away to get properly organised. If they want to do this kind of work, then they should be keen to know more. You can direct them to my first book, Virtually Painless, for an easy read on how to start as a VA (see the Resources section).

There are happily many new VAs who have done their research properly or have done a reputable UK VA training course to learn the ropes. If you are starting small but planning to grow, a new VA is likely to come with more capacity as they build their client base so it could be a good option. It's also worth checking to see if they are accredited by the APVA (Association of Professional Virtual Assistants) or SVA (Society of Virtual Assistants).

What you are looking for is the skills and experience, whether that's employed roles or freelance and that they are professionally set up. Those two things are the key.

Overseas VAs

One of the reasons I wrote this book was because many of the other books out there on working with VAs are not UK-centric. And the UK VA market is different to other countries.

The large majority of UK based VAs are from a PA background, which USA based VAs are often not. I've had many conversations with US based VAs and VA agency owners about this and the consensus is that freelancing in the States is very different because it's hard to charge enough to match a fulltime role that also pays your health insurance and other benefits. Thus, the highly skilled PAs and EAs aren't tempted by a freelance life; they stay employed to get the benefits that gives them.

Often, USA based VAs have a customer service background or fairly basic administration roles and they don't really tend to get the same types of VA roles we do here. Property management and realtor support is a massive market for VAs in the US. Outside of this, there's a real tendency towards low level task churning rather than independent smart business owners. That is a huge generalisation of course, and there absolutely are amazing USA VAs who will work much more like the VAs in this book, as business partners, but you'll pay a sensible UK equivalent rate for those and they can be tricky to find. VAs in the US charging $10 an hour are unlikely to be highly experienced.

The Far East, especially the Philippines, also has a big VA market, mostly serving other countries. And, of course, they are much cheaper to hire than a UK VA because their living costs are so much lower. While I have no doubt many are experienced and capable, I'd exercise a lot of caution when considering hiring an overseas VA. Are they safely set up, tech-wise, to do the work that is needed? Do you have confidence that their English skills will be good enough to handle complex documents and cultural nuances? With so many communications being written in the virtual world, are you happy that their written English is a good reflection of your business as well as in depth enough to build relationships with stakeholders?

While every person is different, an overseas VA may need a lot more training to get up to speed as well as more due diligence to vet them properly and make sure that they are using professional equipment and software. You may have to put in a lot more time and effort to check their work and answer questions.

Chris Ducker, who has huge experience working with and providing Filipino VAs to businesses worldwide, says, "It's not that an overseas VA is incapable or uneducated or won't work hard, but most virtual workers don't think like entrepreneurs – they think like employees".[6]

If you only have low-level tasks, think level one on the delegation scale discussed in Chapter One, then this might be what you need. I'd probably go to automation in the first instance if the tasks really are that simple. But I suspect as well, few of us have fully online business where the only tasks are uploading blogs with a cut and paste or processing an online order. The kind of VAs that will make a huge difference to your business and make a difference to you won't be the handle-turning task-churners. They are the smart, ideas-having, conversation-starting, problem-solving professional business owners that can both get things done and change things for the better. You don't want to be handing tasks out one by one with a video on how to do each thing forever. Don't misunderstand me, I love a Loom video to quickly show someone how to do something, but that's onboarding and then the odd new

---

[6] Chris Ducker, Virtual Freedom: How to work with Virtual Staff to Buy More Time, Become More Productive and Build Your Dream Business

thing. After that period, I'd expect a much more balanced and business to business relationship between client and VA. Yes, tasks need doing, but a VA can learn enough about a business to do a good number of things autonomously after a few months.

Chris Ducker says, "The people that work best with Filipino VAs are online entrepreneurs that have repetitive tasks that need to be handled in a professional, timely fashion. If you expect your Filipino VA to run your business, think again! These brilliant employees are doers not business partners. They'll help you by supporting your business growth, but YOU will need to be the one making plans and executing them!"[7]

And that is why it is worth paying more for a VA if you want deep support. There are other reasons as well. For example, UK VAs are business owners in their own right, operating under many of the same constraints as you are. As such, they'll thoroughly understand issues

---

[7] Chris Ducker (quoted in Jess Ostroff, Panic Proof: How the Right Virtual Assistant can Save Your Sanity and Grow Your Business)

that are potentially going to be relevant in your business, too—like Making Tax Digital, GDPR, and changes to IR35. Most VAs have their finger on the pulse of what is going on in the UK to potentially flag when these types of things come up and whether their client might need to action something.

Most UK VAs also network, which means that when they or their clients need a reliable supplier, they have somewhere to start or people to ask for trusted personal recommendations whether that's to get a website rebuilt or a new logo or just an amazing conference venue near Bristol. If they don't know, they know someone who will! This benefit is much less likely if you hire a VA from outside the UK.

Specialists versus Generalists

VAs come in a multitude of flavours, but you'll find that most have an area where they excel. These are the specialist VAs. Some VAs work with clients in very narrow niches—medical or legal, coaches or creatives, supporting families with personal tasks. Others mainly tackle a particular kind of work—diary management, social media.

True specialist VAs can go deep in their area, to the point where calling them a VA almost disguises their skills. Some specialist VAs could just as easily call themselves a Social Media Manager, an Online Course Specialist, a Web Designer, or a Keap Specialist. Other VAs may specialise in sales funnels, operations management, SEO, copywriting. The list is endless.

Generalist VAs are more likely to offer wide but shallow skills—they can do a lot of tasks just fine but don't tend to niche in any one particular area. As an example, a generalist VA may be more than happy to schedule your social media posts, maybe even research some articles to share, but it is unlikely that they would create your blogs and all your posts. Often a generalist VA will work alongside either a specialist VA or a marketing person so that the marketing person does the complex, high level end (their brilliance) and the VA will schedule the posts.

Bookkeeping is another area where a generalist VA may well do a "light" version, the equivalent of an accounts admin role: sending invoices, reconciliation of those invoices and chasing late payers. Potentially adding bills or expenses to an accounts system. But you wouldn't expect them to do your VAT return or end of year accounts unless they are a qualified bookkeeper or accountant.

It's worth noting that some VAs actively avoid taking on any kind of finance work because of the anti-money laundering regulations mentioned earlier. These regulations mean that most VAs who take on this kind of work must register with HMRC and pay a substantial annual fee to be audited by them. Because of the expense and the hassle, many VAs just avoid this kind of work completely. If you do bring someone onboard who is going to be "in" your finances in any way (more or less), they should ask you for a few documents and proof of ID, much like you have to provide to solicitors when you move house. It's just to make sure you aren't funding terrorism or washing money for the mob.

Working with multiple VAs

So, if different VAs do different things, do you need more than one? It's often a very tidy solution!

Say you're a one-man-band management consultant. You might work with a tech VA to create Survey Monkey surveys and analyse reports as well as build Miro decks for your workshops. Then you might have a diary VA who looks after your day-to-day schedule and gets you where you need to be. Neither does very many hours but they each do what they are best placed to do brilliantly.

I know one business of two people that has a team of eight VAs! They each do different things in the business and work together as team to make sure it all comes together seamlessly. One does customer services, another does diary management, one manages their affiliate marketing, another their website and so on.

My agency has several projects with multiple VAs. Because we specialise in diary management, each team member looks after just two or three people in a large company, so we need multiple VAs to support all the people in the business. Our biggest team is currently 13 VAs, and it is very lucky for us!

Having more VAs doesn't necessarily mean more time and therefore more expense. In many ways, getting someone that knows what they are doing is more cost effective because they are quicker. I can't stress this enough! Potential clients I speak to are often wary of having multiple VAs because it feels like it will cost more. That's not the case—it's about getting the right skills for the right job.

Throwing out your net – where and how do you find your VA?

Now you know what kind of VAs you might come across out there, there are a few ways to find yourself a VA. The best is by personal referral, but this can go horribly wrong in the first few moments that you stick your head over the parapet on LinkedIn and say, "Does anyone know a good VA?" Everyone and his dog will tag every VA they have ever met. That's your first issue. And then they'll suggest their amazing VA who has changed their life… but they're marketing focused, and you need a diary ninja. Perfect for them, absolutely no help to you. You'll be inundated with direct messages and realise that you need a VA just to manage the process of hiring a VA!

So, before you indiscriminately throw your net out, try casting a carefully placed line or two.

Step one: Privately message some of your connections. Something like: "Hi, I'm after some help! I'm looking for a professional and experienced VA to support my coaching business with diary management, travel, invoicing, Mailchimp and other admin for about 20 hours a month. If you know a VA that might be a good fit, I'd love it if you could ask them to email me at dave@davescoaching.com for some more information."

People know people and as long as you are clear on what you need, you might find that is all you need to get some recommendations of people to try. Those people may not be right or may be at capacity, but they may know someone else they could suggest. This feels a little long winded, but personal referral is ideal because people don't suggest anyone that isn't great—it makes them look bad. (Just be aware they may not read your spec, so you may get some left-field suggestions you'll need to filter out.)

Think through your network and send out some messages. Anyone well networked is likely to have come across some generalist VAs, but if you are looking for a whizz on podcasts you'll want to focus on connections who host a podcast and so on.

Step two: If that doesn't work, start looking in places where people like you hang out. Entrepreneurs might look in Start Up groups. Our fictional Dave might be a member of some mastermind groups or coaching groups, maybe even an alumni group from when he did his coaching training. Those people should have a similar business to him so asking for referrals in those groups is a good next step.

The aim is to not make a huge announcement to your entire network until you have exhausted all other opportunities. Everyone will tag everyone, and you'll get a pile of terrible applications so leave this option until last if you've not got what you need through the first approach. Unless you want the publicity, of course.

Getting in applications

Streamline the process and make it really easy to shortlist people or companies that you want to speak to by creating a form that interested parties need to fill in when they first get in touch.

Depending on what your IT set up is, create a form in Microsoft Forms, Google Forms, or Typeform. The form should be fairly straightforward, not a four-page job application! You aren't looking for CVs, many freelancers don't have them. And it certainly isn't the kind of application where you expect to them be listing the last three jobs someone has had. This is simply a way of getting the information you need in one place so you can shortlist companies.

Send your form out to interested parties with a standard message like:

"Hi,

Thanks so much for making contact about VA support. Here's a role description with more information. If you think your business might be a good fit, please complete this form: **LINK** by **DATE** and if we'd like to have a meeting with you, we'll be in touch.

Many thanks
Dave"

And cut and paste that ruthlessly! If you are very tech savvy, you can even automate it....

Then, all your forms will come into one place, and you can review them in a leisurely way and see who you want to have a chat with. At this point it's a numbers game and I'd make the interested folk do the work!

Example VA Shortlist Form

Name:

Business name if different:

Email:

Web page (optional):

LinkedIn Profile (optional):

Instagram page (optional):

Do you have professional indemnity insurance: Yes / No

Are you registered with the ICO: Yes / No / Not applicable

Are you registered with a professional body for anti-money laundering:
Yes/ No / Not Applicable

Having read the role spec, please tell me why your business would be a great fit for mine:

Note: I'd expect a social media VA to have more social presence than a generalist or diary VA and of course you can add or substitute Pinterest, Facebook, Twitter if that is more relevant to your business and the VA support you need.

Note: This AML question is really only needed if there are financial-type tasks on your list that need doing.

Example VA shortlist form.

It's a fine balance between getting the information you need and getting too much. The onus is on them to complete that last box in a way that makes you want to book a call with them. If they don't have much in the way of a website or a LinkedIn profile, then they are going to have to work much harder.

If it is essential that at some point you see your VA in person then do ask for location, but you may well be missing out on amazing support if you stick local, which is a shame for a once-a-year coffee.

Creating a shortlist

Unless something else about them made them 100% perfect, take everyone without insurance straight off the list. They are either very new and don't know what they are doing (yet), or they just aren't set up properly, which is a risk. I'd say they are an easy no.

The next step is to look at their paragraph or two on why they want to work with you in which you asked them to relate back to the role spec you sent them. Do they fit the brief? Did they **read** the brief? Have they taken the time to write a decent amount or just dashed off a couple of sentences? Are there any typos or glaring spelling errors? I know we all make mistakes occasionally; God knows I'm sure there will be many in this book based on my experience of the last one, despite two external proofreads, but this is key. Being virtual, much of what we do and how we interact with people is written. If this person is going to be emailing your clients, what do you want that first impression to be?

Personally, I like to see a bit of personality in a reply, especially if I've shown some of my personality in a job spec. I tend to add something into any ads I have about wanting someone who is going to be fun to work with. It is nice to see that in an application. It's less important if your role is quite task based, but if you are working with someone long term it's great if you gel. If you'll want them to build relationships with people in writing, then it's interesting to see how they use this opportunity to do that.

If you get a four-page novel, that alone may tell you what you need to know. Is it too long? Is it informative or just waffle? Does it answer the question in full, just perhaps a bit too fully, or is it that they've downloaded their entire brain in a panic of "pick me, pick me"? If you like working with people who are detail focused, a longer and fuller reply might well be perfect for your needs; maybe you find shorter ones too crisp and not enough information for you. But there are limits to how much you can read, particularly if they have other places you can read it. If, however, they are having to do some making up for not having much in the way of a website or LinkedIn profile, I might cut them a little slack. And, for the record, several VAs I know have neither a website or an updated social profile anywhere because they are so in demand that they don't need it or have time to do it.

After you've reviewed the main text, hit their website and any social accounts. This is where you're looking for skills. LinkedIn is often an easy place to check past jobs. There's of course the chance that they didn't build their own website and don't do their own social media – we VAs outsource everything but our brilliance as well you know! But I'd be looking for testimonials and reviews from current or past clients, a sensible list of tasks completed (ideally the ones you want them to do!), and again, looking for typos or dead pages or other signs that they aren't attentive to details.

Ideally, get the list down to about six that you want to meet. It's fine if you include some maybes who perhaps didn't quite have enough information but were intriguing. You can always ask them for more information when you connect.

Rate

You'll notice I didn't ask for the VA's rate, or rate range, in the sample application. You certainly can do so if you wish. Asking in the application just runs the risk of you writing them off if they are expensive compared to others that apply and cheap isn't necessarily good! It's worth paying a higher rate as someone experienced is likely to be faster which may well work out cheaper in the end. (I'd be more tempted to write off those that are suspiciously cheap.)

Personally, I tend to talk rates when I am on a call with someone. But applicants may well ask upfront because, quite rightly, they don't want to waste their time applying if you might be one of those clients who thinks that £10 an hour is an acceptable rate. If they ask, you can either say it's negotiable, but you are anticipating it to be in the region of £xx per hour or that you have a budget of £xx per month and that you are happy to discuss if they make the shortlist. You don't want to get into an email back and forth at this point.

Meetings with potential VAs

Once you have your shortlist, you can pop them an email and ask them to book in a time to meet on Zoom or Teams or other online video platform of your choice. I use an online booking system so people can just put a time in my diary, but you can do it old school if that's your thing.

Remember that these are meetings and not interviews. They'll be working out if you are a good fit for them, just as much as you'll be checking if they fit with you. You'll be asking questions of each other. As a note, if you read any of the recommended questions below and think "oh, that's a non-negotiable," then don't wait for the call to ask it—add it to the application form so you aren't wasting time on people that won't work.

Essential meeting questions

Run through this business set-up checklist with every single VA on your shortlist to make sure that they are set up properly:

- Registered as self-employed with HMRC and/or set up as a limited company.
- Professional indemnity insurance.
- Cyber insurance.
- ICO registration if they are based in the UK.
- A data protection policy for their own business AND clear ways of working when it comes to client data – this may form a part of their contract.
- Laptop or desktop set up with paid for anti-virus (even on a Mac) and used only by them, not other members of the family.
- If you are getting them to do anything financial, Anti-Money Laundering (AML) registration. (This again applies only to UK-based VAs. It's a grey area on who needs it and for what. Most VAs that need to be, are supervised by HMRC themselves but registered bookkeepers are usually supervised by their own governing body, same with accountants. Registering for

AML supervision is a paid for service and anyone that has done it will absolutely remember the process! It is not the same as talking to HMRC about setting up as a self-employed person. I'd ask the question only because if they don't know what you are talking about and they do any kind of financial work then they may not be up to date on other business-essential information.)

Other suggested meeting questions

For an individual VA

1. How much capacity do you have a week / month for a new client?
2. What are your normal working hours – ish, I know VAs aren't tied to their desk 9-5 but on a normal day, when are you at your desk?
3. Do you mostly work school holidays? Do you have any planned time off coming up?
4. What do you have in place if there is an emergency? If you are sick, if your laptop broke or you didn't have childcare for three weeks?

5. What kind of people do you love working with?

6. When are you most likely to be satisfied with your work? What about what you do, do you love?

7. How long is your longest client relationship?

8. What's your hourly rate?

9. Do you do retained hours? Is there a discount? Are you VAT registered?

10. Do you have a minimum number of hours per month?

11. Do you record your time on an online timesheet? Is there a client view I can check?

12. What are the next steps if we go ahead?

For an agency or team of VAs

1. Will I have a dedicated VA working with me or is it a bank of VAs and I get whoever is available?

2. How do you decide who on the team is the best match for me based on what you know?

3. What happens if my VA is sick, on holiday or can't work?

4. Do I get a choice of VA or will you select?

5. Will my VA work directly with me or do I send tasks through you?

6. What's your hourly rate?

7. Do you do retained hours? Is there a discount? Are you VAT registered?

8. Do you have a minimum monthly commitment?

9. Do you record your time on an online timesheet? Is there a client view I can check whenever I want or is it just sent monthly?

10. How long is your longest client relationship?

11. What are the next steps if we go ahead?

Some of the questions that they might ask you.

1. Do you have a sense of how many hours you need?

2. How do you like to communicate, are you an email at the end of the day or a one-message-one-task kind of person?

3. What systems do you use? Particularly email.

4. Do you have any particular data or privacy systems that we should be aware of, e.g., special data or a need to use a VPN or similar?

Often all you need is a meeting with someone to know if they are the right fit for you. If you are talking to an agency, you may have a second meeting, possibly two, with the associate that the Lead VA thinks would be a good fit for you. Hopefully there will be a clear winner but if not, you need another loop to go around or to really examine the skills and experience of your top two alongside how they came across and work out which considerations are more vital to you. I would hesitate to make a decision based on cost unless there really is nothing in it in any other way.

It may be at this point that you decide you may need two VAs if you can't find one with all the skills you need — or if you really click with more than one and their skills are complementary. Again, having multiple VAs isn't a route to spending more money. It's often a very sensible and cost-effective way of getting all the skills you need without compromising on quality.

Once a decision is made, but before you sign a service agreement, ask for client references. I always get two. Even though you may have seen testimonials and been personally referred, it is worth asking if they have anyone that could provide a reference. It is just due diligence and a little bit of checking that they are who they say they are. There is a slight chance that client confidentiality may be an issue here; some VA clients prefer people not to realise they use a VA. But I don't think I've ever had a VA say they couldn't provide one, even if one did come from a past employer or a Lead VA, they have done associate work for rather than a direct client.

Contracting

Unless you specify otherwise, I'd expect the VA to be sending you a contract to review and sign. This should lay out what you've agreed and hopefully won't be War and Peace. But do remember that they are running a business, they have their due diligence to do on you, just as much as you do on them! So please be a responsible client, check the contract, read it! And then sign it promptly and pay any deposit or retainer agreed.

A data protection agreement may be part of the contract, or it may be a separate document. Annabel Kaye, the Data and Legal Queen, has the full information on this as part of keeping you, your data and your business safe, so please see the Bonus Chapter at the end of the book to read everything she has to say.

In this chapter we covered lot of ground! We looked at the different types of Virtual Assistant that you might decide to work with. We also covered using your list of tasks to build your own role spec and advert.

Rather than initially putting that advert everywhere and risking being swamped with applications, we considered more strategic places to ask for personal referrals, targeted to the type of support that you are looking for.

Next, we looked at collecting and reviewing applications before holding meetings with your chosen candidates to check the chemistry. At this point your chosen VA will take the lead to a certain degree and get you onboard with their legal paperwork and onboarding process.

This is what we're going to look at in the next section. If you are ready to start getting some brilliance outsourced by your new VA, read on!

***

ACTION STEPS

1. Decide on the commitment you want from your VA – monthly hours or ad hoc.
2. List the skills and experience, and personality that you are looking for in a role spec.
   a. Create a mini version of that as an advert.
   b. Create an online form so you can send out a link to interested parties.
3. Who do you know? Email hand-picked contacts that might be able to recommend someone great.
   a. If that doesn't give you what you need, consider industry specific groups for recommendations.
4. Send out your form and full role spec to interested parties.
5. Shortlist down to people you want to meet.
6. Select your new VA (or VAs)!

Seven

The Nitty Gritty of Working Together

Once you have found your VA, I hope you are excited to get cracking. I'd generally expect the VA to take the lead to a certain extent on what you need to do to get them up to speed. But here's a guide to onboarding new clients based on how we work at Personally Virtual that will give you sense of what to expect.

Getting off to a great start really sets the foundation for your working relationship with your new VA, so don't try and shortcut it in the name of speed. You want this relationship to work, and you want to keep your VA. Put in the legwork.

Onboarding call

Start with an onboarding call that will give your VA a detailed show and tell of what the tasks and relationship look like now, and how you envisage it going in the future.

You must have a thorough understanding of your internal business processes and any client-facing processes before handing tasks over. Some things might be as simple as "what happens when someone gets in touch about a new piece of work they want us to quote on?" and the answer may be a really simple, "I'll email them, cc you and ask you to set up a time for a 30 minute call". Hopefully you used the action steps in earlier chapters to develop thorough lists and unpack all the things you do without thinking about it. Crack out those lists now, because this is the stage to use them as you lay out your current processes to your VA. Think of this conversation as a download of your brain while your new VA gets to grips with how things work. I'd also suggest recording this call on Zoom or Teams so your VA has it to refer back to. Honestly, we are given so much information in these sessions it can, even with the best notes in the world, be a lot to take in!

The other thing to cover in this call is who's who—your main team members, connections, and clients. For a small business this might not be a very long list, for a larger corporation this could be extensive. If you're part of a large organisation, your HR Lead or an EA may meet your new VA to do a more general introduction on the business to maximise your time for the bits that are only relevant to you.

Here's a list of people your VA may need to know about or potentially even be given an introduction to:

Your key clients: Share their names, their role, any useful background on what they are like or how frequently you speak to them and, if they have one, the name of their EA or PA.

Current and imminent projects: Share what your role is, any others on the project team, brief overview of the project and how it's likely to impact the VA. For example:

- We have weekly meetings with Jeff, Sue and Andre, these tend to move about a bit, but they are pretty flexible.
- Or, the project is billed in three parts, the invoice for the first part has gone already, the next is due end of next month but they haven't actually paid the first one yet.
- Or Sara is doing the day-to-day work on this project, I just need to meet her every fortnight to check in and have a monthly call with the client and Sara just to touch base. Next month is all booked but from February they need putting in. Sara is an associate and I'll do an email to introduce you.

Jobs or prospects in the pipeline. For example:

- We're on the shortlist for a project at BT and are waiting for an answer, if we get it, that is likely going to involve some major diary shifts.

- I've been trying to get a meeting in with Arjun at Wallson Capital, he said he had a piece of work for us. We'll have to be as flexible as possible to wedge that into the diary as he wants to start ASAP.

Internal connections: If you have a team, whether freelance or employed, it's really helpful to your VA if you can introduce them once they have an email for your company. Give them a quick run down of who does what as people interact with you. This could be direct reports, mentees, associates or freelance team members.

External suppliers: This could be your web designer, accountant or social media manager. It's useful to know who these people are, even if your VA never needs to interact with them, just so when they see meetings (or invoices) they have a sense of who's who.

Where things are: Where are contact details for people stored? Documents the VA might need? Are there addresses that they should know as standard, e.g., home address rather than a registered address if they are getting things delivered or collected?

Setting up the tech

In an ideal world, your VA should use an email address that is just for you. In most cases, with a MS 365 set up or Google mail this is just a case of adding another user and paying for an additional licence. It is totally worth it for you to have control of what your VA does. I cannot stress this enough. There are some rare occasions when we VAs use our own email, but it doesn't look very professional for you, and it isn't ideal from a security point of view.

If you own their account, you'll be able to access their email if you need to, like if your VA is off sick or on holiday. You'll also then have a permanent record so if in the future you move to another VA, they have all the history and the contacts to search and get some history on. And worst case, it means if something goes wrong you can check what has been sent and to whom.

Ideally, all documents relating to your business owned by your VA should be stored on your storage, whether that's Google Workspace, One Drive, Dropbox or any other system. For similar reasons to the above, you need to have access to their work. The likelihood is that you'll be working on shared documents and you both need to be able to edit them so that's another reason to use a cloud-based solution. If you don't have one and all your files are sat on the C Drive of your laptop, then make migrating them to the cloud a project for your new VA!

There may be other software you use, like Xero or Monday, where you need to add them as a user. If this is your account, add them in. If they are going to set up any kind of software for you, make sure that you are the owner of the account and not them.

We VAs often use password vaults like LastPass or Keeper to store our many passwords. Ideally, you'd share passwords for any sites with us via one of these applications as it allows you to share it so we can access it but not see the password (so no one can accidentally or maliciously change the password on your accounts and lock you out). If that isn't possible, we usually ask that you call us with them or text them separately to the log in email. Please don't email passwords!

Systems training

If you use in your business a bespoke bit of software that your VA is going to need to learn, you'll need to train them up. You'll also need to pay them for the time it takes them to learn.

There are certain fairly generic systems that you would expect everyone to be able to use competently – MS Office, G Suite and document storage systems. If you have something that is fairly common but not universal, then you probably want to hire a VA that already has knowledge of that system. But if your perfect VA is just missing that one skill and it's not the most complex system in the world, you might make the call and accept that they'll need to upskill a little on your time.

Most experienced VAs are adept at picking up new software. Project and task management systems as well as CRMs shouldn't need a lot of training. If you've used one, you can usually pick up the others fairly fast. Your

VA may just need guidelines on how you prefer to use it as everyone will have their own processes, customisations and ways of working on a given system.

Crack on!

Once you've had your call with your new VA, they have an email address and access to all the tech they need, you're doing it! This can be the slightly weird bit. All of a sudden, you have someone who can do things for you. Here are three tips to help you get off on the right foot.

First and foremost, pace yourself! We're here to work, make no mistake. But literally dumping everything on your to do list onto a new VA at once is a bad move.

Reorganising and tidying your whole One Drive and emailing the accountant for a meeting about year-end figures are unlikely to be equal in terms of when they need doing and how important they are to the running of your business. Yes, we all have a One Drive that looks like Satan vomited in it, but honestly no one will die if it takes another month to sort it out – I suspect it's been on your list since you first moved everything over from

Dropbox in 2018 and as yet, no one has suffered anything worse than a mild irritation and 12 versions of the same document not having been properly archived. So, look at your list of tasks with your new VA and agree which things need doing ASAP, which are regular tasks and when they need doing and then create a wish list of things that it would be good to cross off eventually. Prioritise, explain and plan.

If you're still tempted to drop a task list with us and run, please don't. It's terrifying being a VA some days. We don't really know you or your business yet. We are highly unlikely to be able to prioritise a list of 450 things you've just landed on our laps. We are only booked for 20 hours a month, this is 50 hours of work right here! When do you expect it by? Where do I start? Half of this makes no sense without more context. If you want to give your new VA a nervous breakdown or send them into the "New Client Horrors" you are doing a grand job. (See the New Client Horrors section later under FAQs).

Calm down. Take a breath.

Not only is it good to prioritise, it's also best to start with assigning the VA just a few tasks off your list. I don't mean like the lovely old chap who once had me type three lines into a spreadsheet to prove I could do it. (That is a whole different story but given he didn't know what a spreadsheet was until I'd created one for him, it was pretty grim.) But do start with some relatively simple tasks or some regular tasks and then review. As you and your VA get more confident with each other, build up.

Second, once you have a VA, you have to communicate with them. Otherwise, they can't do stuff. I know that sounds like a radical concept but as we've already established, although we're great, we aren't psychic. You need to give us work to do. Email us! Turn up to meetings that we put in with you to talk about work.

Based on my survey of VAs across the UK, 16% of VAs have had a client sign up and then ghost them—never to be seen or heard from again. The client is keen as mustard, sometimes they even sign the contracts, often even pay out cold hard cash, and then, poof, they are gone. Like they never existed. And man, it's frustrating!

We want to get cracking, make life easier and do stuff and you are missing in action. Where are you?

There are times when people get so busy that it's hard for them to delegate, but if there is anyone that you should communicate with so you can offload some work, it's us!

Sometimes these vanishing clients are part of a bigger team so we can perhaps talk to their mentor or others on their project and, you know, check they are still alive. But if it's a one-to-one relationship and we only have you to communicate with and you are the lesser-spotted jungle cat-client, we're stuffed.

And, with a slow stuttering start like this, it's pretty challenging to then get going properly. If you don't give us any work, we can't add any value, then you don't see the point of having a VA, and so the relationship breaks down before it even started.

Third, when you take on a VA you must commit to making time for them. Not loads. Even ten minutes a day to reply to queries and send over a few tasks is good. You can find ten minutes a day. Even five, we'll take five.

Of course, if you've taken the time to read this book, you'll have learnt that in order to succeed with a VA you are going to have to put in some effort. It's vital that you make time upfront to get this thing going, or it will not get going and you will not get any help. I know it feels quicker and easier at this point to do things yourself for the sake of speed but that isn't going to help you long-term.

As Michael Hyatt says, "Empower your virtual assistant to help you. They can't will that to happen; you have to be willing to let go of some tasks."[8]

---

[8] Michael Hyatt, The Virtual Assistant Solution: Come up For Air, Offload the Work you Hate, and Focus on What you do Best

Agree ways of working

Now that we've established you aren't going to vanish or overload your VA with enough tasks to keep a whole army busy for a fortnight, let's look at the details of how it should be done. All this guidance hinges on—you guessed it—good communication.

Clarify your expectations around tasks

You can't assume that your VA knows what you mean when you give them a task unless you are really clear, particularly in the early stages. When assigning a task, you should cover things like:

- What's the overall objective?
- When do you need it by?
- What form should it take (an email, a spreadsheet, something else)?
- If it's open-ended, give a guide on how long to spend on a particular task ("see how far you get in an hour and let me know").
- If there are preferred suppliers to buy things from, name them.

- Be clear that the VA can come back and ask more questions if they have them or get help. Tell them you'll assume no news from them means that they have everything they need to get this done.
- For larger projects, add check in points or ask your VA for a regular update. This might be at your weekly meetings (described below) or it might take another form, but you don't want to lose sight of the project for weeks at a stretch without some information on the status.

Once you've given your VA the information above, you can leave them to do the work without micromanaging them. If they miss a review point, or if what they send you is way off the mark, check in and make sure that they're clear what is needed. One perfect place to check in is on weekly calls.

Communication

"The single biggest problem in communication is the illusion that it has taken place." George Bernard Shaw

Here is a very short version of this section if you are low on time: **Communicate, communicate, communicate and be respectful.**

That's it. That's the fundamentals of how to work with a VA right there.

As Michael Hyatt says in The Virtual Assistant Solution, "When it comes to virtual assistants, there's no such thing as over-communication. It's easy to say, but it's also easily overlooked for the sake of time and urgency. Listen: if your spouse can't read your mind after however many years of marriage what makes you think your virtual assistant can?"[9]

Where a VA-Client relationship struggles, it's almost always because the client hasn't communicated, either at all, enough, sensibly, or regularly. Or they have no

---

[9] The Virtual Assistant Solution: come up for Air, Offload the Work you Hate, and Focus on What you do Best, Michael Hyatt

respect for boundaries in time or in paying promptly, i.e., they are disrespectful.

We are blessed these days with almost too many channels of communication, so you'll need to agree with your VA when to use what. But you must use something!

Weekly calls

It's best practice to hold weekly calls for you and your VA to work through your lists together and keep work moving forward. They are billable time. They may only be 15 minutes once your VA is established, but they are vital. These calls let us ask questions about things on your list, check priorities if meetings need to move around, review a couple of options on flights and so on. We'll update you on and get your decisions about ongoing projects or events that we're managing.

For folks with a diary VA, there might be a canter through the diary for the next couple of weeks so we can check you've got everything you need in terms of prep time, location information and so on. We can work out how to resolve clashes where we need your input on what takes priority, and we can review anything else that you might have coming up in future weeks that we need to start planning for.

For some people, the weekly call might entail a review of a CRM system and a number of prospects that they are trying to book meetings with. Many VAs hold their clients to account on these types of things that have a tendency to slip off the list when things get busy. We can review the sales pipeline every week to see what's coming and who might need a chase, and whether you're doing the chasing or we are.

Communication outside meetings

Clearly, you're likely to communicate with your VA outside of your weekly meeting. You should both agree upfront how this communication might take place and when. In other words, get detailed not just on what you want to communicate, but on *how* and *how often* you want to communicate. This will vary for everyone based on their preferences and it is entirely possible that you may start off and realise it isn't quite working so you need to tweak it. And this adjustment is the kind of thing you'd talk about at your regular meetings.

As an example, this is the system I have with my VA Helen. In my business I have emails, Slack, Teams, Click Up and a phone so it's key that we don't drive each other crazy with messages all over the place that we lose track of. Remember that communication works both ways— you also need to respond to things, or your VA can't get their work done.

What are we discussing	When do you need me to see this?	Where should we discuss it?
Something Helen is stuck on that's time sensitive	ASAP	WhatsApp
Kathy has an urgent question	ASAP	WhatsApp
Notes, questions or things to review on ongoing projects	Within 24 hours	ClickUp, on the tasks that it relates to
New tasks that Kathy wants Helen to pick up	Within 24 hours	ClickUp, in Ops chat if not task related or added as a subtask with date on an existing task
Something already on an email	Within 24 hours	Email, potentially with notes added to ClickUp where appropriate
Weekly timesheet task	Not urgent	Helen will email

Table of communication.

Note that there isn't a response time on these, just when something needs to be seen. An urgent WhatsApp may contain an urgent task, but I rarely have any. You'll also see that although we have access to both emails and Slack, they aren't used over-much. Where things start on email with a conversation, we'll keep them there. This maybe a change to client hours or associate conversations so I'll probably have emailed the client or associate and copied Helen in. But I never email Helen a task or a question because we've agreed that ClickUp is the best option for us both to manage tasks. She sends me one email a week which is a specific task she completes.

Your system doesn't have to look like mine, it almost certainly won't. It just needs to work for both you and your VA, so agree with your VA on the when and how of your various modes of communication. And stick to it! If you find it isn't working a few weeks in, have a conversation about it and adjust it.

Here are a few of the ways you and your VA may choose to communicate.

Voice memos

Calling your VA with everything will interrupt their work every single time, which isn't ideal. If you know that you are better at downloading your brain verbally, a sensible system is to use a Voice Memo or Voice note app on your phone and then send your VA the recordings by email or to a task system. You can also dictate an email or record a voice note in Telegram or WhatsApp. You can use voice memos to help your VA reply to more complex emails, to add things to their task list and to give them updates. This way you can work in a way that suits you without compromising your VA's need to work on other things. It also means you don't need to factor in time zones or whether you're working late at night.

Videos

A really good way to show someone how to do something is by recording your screen as you do a task. There are plenty of free apps out there that give you up to five minutes free, which is plenty for a quick tutorial. I tend to use the Loom extension on Google Chrome. Showing someone how to do something live is great but they don't have anything to refer back to. A short video showing how to do something—for example how to create a new client on the CRM and set up the new client automation—will be a permanent record that's useful for both you and your VA. I suggest you create a training folder and label everything clearly so you can both find things again. This also helps you build up a training library for the future.

Task management systems

A shared task list is a gamechanger. If you don't have a task management system, you might well ask your VA to set one up as one of their tasks! Even if you already keep a Google Doc or a spreadsheet of tasks, you might consider levelling up to something less messy. There are some brilliant options out there, for free, that you can use to efficiently collaborate with your VA.

The beauty of a task or project management system is that everyone knows where they stand. You can see what has been done, you can both add notes if needed. With one client I'd add a tag to every task she added once I picked it up, so she knew that I was on the case. This is a slightly more hi-tech version of the "got it" email or thumbs up to acknowledge receipt of something.

Some people like their VA to send them an update at the end of every week (some of the more detail focused amongst us, every day) and that's great IF you need that and IF you are going to read it. Bear in mind, the time it takes your VA to pull together this list of what's where is billed to you. So if it is going to take 30 minutes a week and you only look at it once a month that is a lot of wasted money.

By using a task system you'll be able to see in real-time what tasks are still outstanding and what are in progress or not started, depending on the system you use.

If your business already uses a task system, add your VA. Create an area for the two of you to share that is purely for VA stuff. You may of course be adding them in to other tasks across the business but make sure there is an area where you can clearly see just the things your VA is working on. It's easier for you both to have that dedicated space.

If you don't know where to start on a task system, ask your VA. Chances are they will have a favourite and will be able to set you up and show you the ropes. I am a task system obsessive and have tried an awful lot of them over the years. In fact, I've probably tried so many in the pursuit of productivity that ironically, I've wasted hours of my life. But that's my issue to deal with! I'm going to indulge my nerdiness in the Resources Section and talk about a few of my favourites. Some are free, some cost and some are free but with paid extras. See the Appendix for this quick run down of apps. They are all running at the timing of writing and there may well be more, even more brilliant ones out there that your new VA can introduce you to.

Ad hoc phone calls

Generally speaking, outside any scheduled check ins most VAs only expect clients to call if there is an imminent crisis or someone has lost a limb. I actively discourage it! I'm concentrating on what I'm doing, if it's not urgent, don't interrupt me.

There are some caveats to that. If you have an utterly insane schedule and your VA needs to speak to you, we'll kind of take what you can give us and if that means you call while waiting for a plane, so be it. And it may be that we take that unscheduled call from the sofa or the school playing field watching football. That's the risk you take when you ring someone on a whim. So it's not ideal really, as they may not have their notes to hand or their laptop but as long as you're relaxed about that, we can be too if that is what has been agreed.

Remember that calls are billable, whether planned or not. And potentially might be billed extra if they fall out of hours. It'll depend on your contract.

A good rule to get into is to only call your VA if it's urgent. That way, when you call, we will mostly likely pick up because you last phoned us off schedule 18 months ago, therefore something is urgent. If you ring twice a week and it isn't urgent on any of those times, there's a chance we'll eventually just let your calls go to voicemail in an effort to train you better! However, that call, even unanswered and going to voicemail, has distracted us from what we are doing. So try not to do it, please! If you must "speak" then send a voice note.

WhatsApp

When you think about what communication channels you have in your business, consider if it's sensible for your VA to be on it. Beware of giving access to too much. Firstly, for security reasons but also, if there are 47 things that need to be read but only one of them needs your VA to know it or action it, that is a lot of wasted time for your VA checking all the messages for the one key one.

For whatever reasons, WhatsApp seems to be a particularly common tool for this kind of VA time suck. A client once added me to their business WhatsApp group, and I lasted all of two days before I told them I was coming off it. Unless I read every message, I didn't know if it was an action for me. And for me to read every message on this insane group was costing them two hours a day of my time. Utter lunacy. And they were based globally so this thing went off at all hours. I never felt like it went away.

Check with your VA about their thoughts on WhatsApp. For some, WhatsApp messages will be the equivalent of a phone call—an urgent thing. Others routinely use

WhatsApp for correspondence with clients and are fine with it. Some VAs have a business WhatsApp account and have tools to manage it really well and it forms a key part of their communication methods.

Slack / Teams / Google Chat / Instant Messages

All of these are fabulous communication tools for teams and can be great to use with your VA. Again though, don't add them to team channels or groups "for information" if there might one day be a task buried in a whole stream of messages. Consider putting in a rule that if you need your VA to read or action something, you will @ them. Otherwise, they can safely ignore the rest and only need to check the small handful of notifications and not the 17 pages of text before that.

Whatever version of instant message or collaboration tool you have in your business (if any) needs to be factored into your communication plan in a similar way.

Email Communication

Most VA-client partnerships use email as the main form of communication and there is a reason for that: it's fantastic. You can add attachments, copy people both internally and externally.

There is an art to writing an email and it's not easy. (There are many, many books on writing emails to help. Personally, Kim Arnold is my go-to; see Resources at the back of this book.) Much of what you put in an email will depend on who you are sending it to and why. Problems arise when VAs are copied into an email, but our action isn't clear.

Here are some examples.

Bad email: "Hi Jeff, great to hear that you are thinking about starting that project. I'd love to get a time in to talk about it". This is vague and leaves no one with a clear action, including the prospective client, Jeff!

Better email: "Hi Jeff, great to hear that you are thinking about starting that project. I'd love to get a time in to talk about it, can you liaise with Vicki, cc'd, to find a time in my diary".

Looking at the email, without a code, or a standard procedure, there is no way to know whether or not the VA should follow this up. If I were the VA reading it, I'd think "ah ha, a new bit of business, if I don't hear in 24 hours, I'll follow up" but not every exec wants that. Unless you have a system. And then do you follow up once? Twice?

Best email: "Hi Jeff, great to hear that you are thinking about starting that project. I'd love to get a time in to talk about it. Vicki looks after my diary; I'll ask her in copy to send over some times next week".

Isn't that a clearer task? It's an immediate action point with no ambiguity. It gives Vicki a timeline, which gives her a steer on urgency. And Jeff, the would-be client, can relax knowing that the next step isn't down to him.

Copying in a VA is a great way to pass on tasks. We can take it from here, find out if there's a PA at the other end, we can work with for slots etc. We can then let you know when it goes in, check if you want any prep time etc.

Many PAs and VAs have a code with the person they support which massively reduces the need to follow up an email—consider creating one of your own with your VA. These are great for a signal to the VA of what is to be done. A secret language if you will. Here are some examples I've seen used.

"Thanks so much for getting in touch. I'd love to have a meeting with you. My diary is pretty maxed at the moment with some overseas trips, but Vicki will find a slot"

This is code for "absolutely not the least bit important. Stick it in a month out and if it has to move in the future for something else, that's fine"!

"Thanks so much for getting in touch. I'd love to have a meeting with you. Let me know when works and we'll do our best to accommodate this" is code for *really important meeting, needs to go in ASAP and if we have to move stuff, let's talk about what we can kick out of the diary*".

A note on tone

There are many ways you can communicate with your VA, but tone is always important. You'll agree over time what style works for you.

I remember laughing really hard when a newish client wrote me a formal email every time she needed something doing.

Hi Kathy,

I hope you're well.

Can you please find some time in the next two weeks for me to meeting with Sophie and Priya? 45 mins ideally or if we can't make that work, 30 would probably be ok. Sophie doesn't work Wednesdays.

Many thanks
Sarah

I love that she was courteous enough to write that, it's certainly better than going the other way, snapping orders like a drill sergeant. However, we then had a chat about how I'm meant to be saving her time and we introduced a task system whereby she wouldn't feel the need to be quite so polite! The above request added to Todoist would probably be:

45 mins (or 30) w Sophie and Priya, next two weeks. Thanks!

The moment I look at Sophie's diary I'll see she doesn't work Wednesdays, so I didn't need that extra information.

The opposite of Sarah's very nice email is the snappish tone. Everyone has worked with someone who has no concept of their written tone. Or worse, they just don't care when you aren't perceived as important.

When you write things down you need to think how it will be read. As Virtual Assistants we know this more than most. We're experts; 95% of our communication is written, so we work at it. We don't get to see the fluffy side of you that might be totally apparent in the office to everyone else. All we see is the what-feels-quite-pissy email reply to a question that just says "no, that won't work." I've had VAs on the team quit because of people's written tone.

There's no excuse not to be polite. I mean if you know you sound rude because you're insanely busy and you can't manage more than three-word replies, at least add an emoji to soften it. You can do that in email now, even Microsoft is helping those who have a poor email manner. It's frustrating for us because we know you are perfectly capable of writing a nice email to a client or a prospect. You just can't be bothered to afford us the same courtesy. And that makes us a little bit grouchy. We're business partners, not minions. We don't need a novel, but a "thanks" or even a "ta" or a "tx" has never gone amiss. Stick a kiss on the end if you really must.

It's still your business

Now that you've outsourced some of the things that happen in your business, you need to find a way to keep on top of what is happening. It can be extremely odd going from doing everything and knowing everything to things going on without you doing them! Some people find it very disconcerting.

Even if you love the feeling of freedom your VA brings, this is still your business—so you'll need to put in place some systems to ensure that you have an overview of what is happening (without being in the weeds of the details) and to communicate that with others in the team.

Using a task management or project management system, as discussed in detail above, will really help give you an overview of the current status of tasks. You may not use this for everything, it may purely be for internal tasks: invoicing, organising an event, getting new office furniture ordered. Or it may capture everything in your business. It doesn't matter how you do it, but it's key that you know what is happening in your business, who is responsible for what and when it's happening. You'll also be having those weekly updates with your VA to review any ongoing projects and for each of you to check in on anything that is needed.

I'd also recommend that once your VA or VAs are settled, they create and keep updated an operations manual that lays out how everything works that they touch on. If you were a diligent reader and you did your work upfront creating the Bible of You, it could be a starting point for your VA to build on. The operations manual might not be a written document, it might be a series of screen shots or videos or a flow chart. Whatever is the easiest for you both and is the best way to make sense of the information.

We have our VAs create an ops manual or cheat sheet for any clients that they work on. For us, this means that if they had an accident or couldn't work, someone else has a hope of being able to understand their tasks and their role. I would suggest that you ask your VA to create a similar document for you once they've been in place for three months or so. And it should be updated regularly.

You need to know that if they vanished or were ill, that you know where things are, what tasks they do and how to pick them up. It sounds crazy now, you know all the tasks in your world. But a good VA will be gradually working to reduce the number of things you need to get involved with and will create systems and reminders for themselves to get things done. And you need to know what they are and how to do them should that VA leave or not be able to work. You don't want to not know what happens in your business! That doesn't mean at all that you need to see every single thing, but there should be a record somewhere that includes what your VA does, how and when. A shared password system is also very useful to make sure that you have access to everything that you might need.

In a larger business with multiple VAs, in addition to an ops manual you might have a backup VA for every business area so someone else always knows the ropes of each role.

Where my agency supports bigger, corporate clients with a large team of VAs we'll have many documents to lay out information about the business and then individual documents on each area or person we support. There are plenty of us to cover one another across the team if we need to. And when there is a planned holiday, handover notes are always done. It will depend on the business areas but these have been known to be the size of a novella or it can be two lines. Either might be appropriate.

In addition, your VA should be able to send you a substitute if they go away or can't work. Having something concrete for someone else to pick up when that happens is very helpful and will make you feel much more comfortable about having a sub.

Endings

There will come a point when your working relationship with your VA comes to an end, whether that is your decision or theirs. There are all manner of reasons for this. Indeed, one of the excellent reasons for working with a VA rather than an employee is that when you need to switch up or out, it's contractually and financially a lot easier. Most VA contracts will specify a notice period and you may still need to pay if you are on a retainer; this gives the VA some protection if a big client just changes their mind overnight. Check the contract that you have with your VA.

In this section we look at the various reasons why this might happen and how best to transition to either a new VA, a PA, or something else depending on what is needed. I very much hope that your relationship with your VA is such that you can include them in your thinking and handover (obviously that might not work in the case of underperformance). Some VAs even recruit their successors.

Increased volume of work

With any luck, your business or role is booming and you need more support than your current VA can provide.

Start by having a conversation with your VA to see if it's a role that could be split and whether adding another VA in (whether they find a subcontractor or you find an additional VA) might be the answer. The "original" VA might continue to pick up the high level and more complex work and will delegate the easier routine tasks to a new VA, whether that's travel bookings, series of meetings, expense receipts, minute taking or whatever. The added advantages of this are a) you don't have to lose your VA's skills and experience, b) the original VA will do much of the work of managing the new person day to day so you don't have to, and c) this system provides built in holiday cover when the lead VA is away. If that will give you enough hours and your original VA is up for it, it can be a neat solution. Especially if you have a brilliant Lead VA you don't want to lose!

There is a tipping point at which it will be more cost effective to employ someone to take over from your VA, however. If you remember the section on hours, most VAs won't bill any more than 20-30 hours a week. So if that is the amount you are using, that's pretty much equivalent to a fulltime role. If you need that amount of time or more dedicated to you, it is possibly time to move to an employed PA or EA. It's worth sitting down and doing some maths to see if you've reached the point where an employee would be more cost effective. Remember the hourly pay for a PA is very different to a VA. You have to pay them whether or not they are working and you'll also need to pay NI and tax and cover holidays, sickness etc. You will also need to provide them with safe working equipment as it is your responsibility as their employer to make sure that they have a safe set up – both for your business and for their health.

If you can be open and honest with your VA about the changes it will really be appreciated. If you have a great relationship then get them involved in recruiting if they are happy to – they will be a helpful input to finding the right person to take over. Depending on contractual arrangements they may be able to stay and do a full handover so you have an overlap of time to make the move as painless as possible. Or, if the VA has had to find new clients, then you might well be able to pay them on an ad hoc basis to come back and do a handover.

The end of a working relationship can be tricky timing-wise so the more open both sides can be and the more helpful each can be to the other the better. From your point of view, you want a seamless transition, but the VA is losing hours – potentially a lot of hours if you are having to employ someone because of the volume of work. They are going to need to replace those billable hours with as small a gap as possible. Remember, if they aren't on the clock, they aren't earning. They will be needing to line up their next client or clients to replace your hours on their books. If you've had a great relationship with them up to now, there is no reason that it can't continue. Open conversations and as much notice as possible go a long way to easing the pain of losing a big client. You can also perhaps recommend your VA to your contacts, offer to write a LinkedIn post singing their praises or at the least do a thorough testimonial or case study and put reviews wherever your VA would like them. And if you really like them, send a gift or a handwritten card to thank them.

I always think that a client needing to move to a fulltime PA is a measure of our success as well as the client. We've proved what a valuable resource a PA can be! It's my favourite kind of moving on. The client is growing— it's a business decision. Whilst it certainly can be a pain replacing the hours, as endings go, it's brilliant. No hard feelings, only success all around. The door is never closed, it's always ajar as you've made a wonderful new contact. I'm still in touch with many of my past clients, and we still cheerlead each other's successes, make mutual recommendations where it is appropriate and have the odd virtual coffee to stay connected. There's no point in burning bridges on either side.

Your VA gives notice

There are any number of reasons why this might happen. If you aren't clear why your VA has given notice then it's worth asking. Feedback is a gift!

Where I've given notice after a long time, it's usually been agonised over for months and will almost certainly be purely a business decision. For me, if I don't like working with you, you'll be gone very fast! Some VAs are more tolerant, but my "no Sunday-horrors" rule kicks in instantaneously. If it isn't fun, I won't be doing it.

We VAs have a careful balance of clients and we juggle them. And sometimes, one client doesn't quite fit into that juggling anymore. This is rarely personal. More often than not it's a decision based on a number of different levers that the VA is pulling to get the right balance of work on their plate.

Based on my survey of VAs across the UK, here are the reasons (in order of frequency) for having to give notice to a client.

1. I didn't like the work or find it enjoyable.
2. They were overly demanding and didn't respect my boundaries.
3. They were chaotic and couldn't manage themselves, let alone me.
4. They weren't nice to work with
5. The hours were too few and it was "bitty".
6. They were poor payers / paid late / never paid.
7. I had to chase them constantly and it was annoying.
8. The type of work I wanted to do changed and they weren't a good fit for me any more.
9. They constantly nit-picked on hours spent or complained about hours / costs.
10. They didn't respect me or the role and/or belittled my work and abilities.

11. We just weren't a great working partnership - we didn't gel.
12. My working hours / situation changed and they were next on the list (e.g. less billable time available or I moved and they needed someone nearby).
13. I couldn't help them and it was frustrating (whatever the reason).
14. They wouldn't take a price increase.
15. I just got a better offer elsewhere and they were next on the list to go.
16. The hours got too much for me.

Whilst this isn't the biggest survey, I think that the results are interesting. The subsequent question was based on how often clients demonstrate these behaviours – paying late, ignoring boundaries etc and they happen quite rarely. Which tells me that VAs don't tolerate working with people that aren't a good fit, they make the decision to move on.

As a client, what you can take from this is that if you behave badly (items 2, 3, 4, 6, 7, 9, and 10) then your chances of being fired increase quite dramatically. I would also take from this the massive plus that if you are great to work for, your VA will stick around, potentially even if the work or money isn't the best fit! It is a good reminder that when you work with freelancers they too have the choice of who they work with and why.

Some of the responses to the survey included:

"I took on a project to setup and update a business's social media pages, they refused to pay on time, tried calling me on weekends and out of hours, complained when I refused a meeting at 22.00, and never provided me with the information I required on time, delaying the project. They then complained about the delay. It was a pure nightmare from start to finish and I was glad to walk away."

"I have good relationships with all my clients. If I didn't get on with a client or if they gave me the 'Sunday shivers' I'd get rid of them immediately (like the one who kept calling me during my friend's funeral)".

Asking VAs to pick their ideal client characteristics, the top five items were:

1. A nice person to work with, I get on with them.
2. Interesting work.
3. Someone happy to pay my rates without haggling.
4. Gives me independence to do the work my way.
5. Thinks of me as one of the team and part of their business.

The good news is that you have full control over the top characteristic on that list. So even if your work isn't that thrilling, that isn't as essential to a VA as you being a nice client to work with.

Not enough work

Small jobs are annoying. I'm sorry, but it's true. On the survey above it was the fifth most likely reason a VA moved on from a client.

If you aren't sending enough work to your VA to make it worth their time, whether due to a tiny budget or your own difficulty delegating, you will be on the hit list for being fired. It's a risk you're taking. There comes a point where we can't keep chasing you for work. If you are just sending us odds and sods of work here and there it's a distraction from bigger clients and fiddly and there will come a point where it's not worth the admin of sending you an invoice. It's also frustrating not being able to do more. As a little client, when something bigger and better comes in, you are top of the hitlist. Which is why it's really key to make sure you don't outsource to a VA until you have enough work that it's worth everyone's time.

The work is not fun or interesting or not my thing any more

Not all work is equal. Some tasks are more fun than others and if your work isn't as much fun as someone else's, then that makes it more at risk. And fun varies from person to person. This is part of why getting the right VA for your tasks is vital – an ops and start up expert VA is going to get bored doing 90% diary management, and a diary VA won't find much excitement doing data entry. Maybe it isn't so much the tasks themselves as the other people we're interacting with day to day. I certainly had one client who was lovely, but her clients were totally awful, and it made me miserable dealing with them daily. Clearly, she's not going to fire her clients to make my day better! So, if I need to create space or something better comes along, that job is going to move to the top of my "get shot" list.

As we progress into VA-dom, we grow and change. What we didn't used to mind when we first started because we needed the work, we perhaps wouldn't pick to do five years into freelance life. And whilst we'll still do it for you for a time out of loyalty, there will come a point when seven hours of data entry a month isn't going to be our first choice. And we may have niched into specific types of work after a few years of learning and developing our skills and we want to focus on that. My business now bears no resemblance to its early days and because of that, I have let some clients go. Some things are just not the best fit for me and I'm lucky enough now to have the luxury of deciding how I want to spend my days.

The client won't pay current rates

Inevitably, VAs have to increase our rates from time to time. It isn't something that any business does lightly. Our rates are what the market will pay, so it's possible that, if our rates to an existing client are going up, new clients will already have been paying that rate for a considerable period of time. And it may be that we are now out of your budget. It happens. And most often we will accept that and if you ask us to, we'll help find and onboard a replacement.

If you just don't want to pay the new rates, then you'll need to move on to someone else. We have a limited number of billable hours in a day and we need them to be most the profitable they can be. Much as we may love you, our business head will eventually overrule our soft side. Mutual love and respect sadly doesn't pay off a mortgage.

Too much work

Again, this is all about the ceaseless juggle of billable hours. It's pretty rare that we'd give notice to a client because it's too busy but there are some reasons why too busy isn't good! If we started with a set number of hours and it crept up this can be a challenge if we're already fully booked up. Our other issue with larger clients is that it can be risky having all your eggs in one basket. Spreading our time over multiple clients ensures that if one moves on elsewhere, we still have a decent client base. If we're spending 80% of our time on you, potentially that's a risk as you may move to a fulltime PA. It's even more of a challenge if you aren't paying full rate.

It just isn't working

This is kind of a cop out – the "it's not you, it's me" equivalent in VA-Client terms. But this is usually sussed out pretty early on. Sometimes, this is the New Client Horrors (see the FAQ section) but sometimes it generally just isn't a good fit personality-wise and it takes a couple of weeks for that to be apparent. Occasionally, working styles do not align and if that is the case and it's terminal, it is as well to know early.

As with any relationship, there are nuances. While you might be a perfect client for one VA, you won't be for another. This is why when I walked you through finding a VA we looked at personality types as well as skills.

You are not a good client

If your VA hasn't given any of the reasons above for why they are letting you go, you may not be the easiest to work with, otherwise known as "a pain in the butt". I'm sorry to be the bearer of bad tidings but the survey results are pretty clear: VAs don't want or need to work with difficult people.

If you are really brave and want to know, ask. Because there's a strong chance if you have driven one VA to the point of sacking you off, your next one won't find you any easier to work with. Maybe something outside of your control happened meaning it was the wrong time to have started working with a VA and it just went totally pear-shaped as you couldn't commit enough time to it? Maybe a VA is not the right solution for you, and you'd be better with someone in the office? Perhaps you need to do some self-development and get some coaching around your communication style or organisational abilities before outsourcing is a realistic option for you?

In Summary

I hope that now you have some excellent knowledge to take forward into your new VA relationship.

Communication is the key to a great client / VA partnership. Working out the best methods of communication for you and your VA will be the most important element of your relationship as great communication makes life easy and poor communication (or lack of communication or communication in too many channels) can cause frustration and confusion.

Do your onboarding thoroughly and ensure that your VA is given all the tech access and training that they need to understand you and your business. When delegating to a VA you need to plan, prioritise and explain. Agree a system of managing tasks between you (see also Appendix 1 for some ideas on task systems).

We also looked at the ending of your VA relationship. At some point you and your VA will part ways, even if that is when you retire! It's worth thinking about future planning from the start of your working relationship with a VA, simply to make it easier when that time comes. It's also sensible to have your business documented in the event of a crisis and your VA can help you do this.

Are there any burning questions still lurking in your mind? I hope not, but just in case, turn to the next chapter for the answers to more questions and concerns that I've heard time and again over the years.

***

ACTION STEPS

1. Onboard your new VA and download your brain!
    a. Explain your role, your work, your key clients, stakeholders and colleagues.
2. Get your new VA a bespoke email address for your business as well as access to any systems they need.

    a. If you have any systems that require it, get them trained up.

3. Manage your task list.

    a. Prioritise, explain and plan.

    b. Delegate tasks clearly – what is the deadline, expected output, preferred supplier or time budget?

4. Communicate

    a. Agree your communication methods and review your emails to see if the implied task is clear.

    b. Review regularly how you both feel communication between you is working.

5. Document

    a. Once Your VA is settled in, ensure that they are documenting what they do so that there's always a record of how they work should it be needed.

Eight

FAQs and Fears

How many hours is the minimum to use a VA?

I'm going to hedge my bets here and say "it depends". It will depend on the VA as some have minimum requirements. And it will depend on how much you need to accomplish. We typically say that any less than eight hours a month isn't enough for someone to make a difference but others may say ten or twenty hours or even more.

How much is it going to cost me?

And the million-dollar question – how much does a VA cost an hour? Again, it depends. Just as there are some PAs and admin support that are relatively junior, there are levels of VA experience.

According to the 2023 SVA survey[10], the current mean average rate for a UK VA is £29.77 per hour. I'd be highly dubious about anyone in the UK charging less than £30 per hour. But the top end can be up to £50, even £100 per hour for highly experienced specialised VAs. Some VAs are also VAT registered so you'll need to take that into consideration if your business isn't registered for VAT.

I'm a little (in fact a lot) behind in my admin, is a VA going to judge me?

Well, maybe a little. But don't worry too much about it — we all have guilty piles of something we should be doing but can't get around to. I confess, my personal

---

[10]: UK Virtual Assistant Survey 2023 (SVA) - for more information please visit
www.societyofvirtualassistants.co.uk

filing pile is shameful and has not been touched in nearly a year. We all have things that we'd love to be better organised.

I've been handed carrier bags stuffed with receipts and been shown inboxes with 40,000 unread emails. I've seen people years late on VAT returns. At this point, not much fazes me and I certainly think we VAs love a challenge!

As my amazing VA Helen says, "One business owner's frog is another Virtual Assistant's Freddo - easily devoured with plenty of room for more."

And this lovely quote from our survey sums up a typical VA attitude: "Don't feel bad about giving us that huge inbox to detox and calendar to untangle - it's what we're here for and we love making your working day easier for you!".

How do VAs purchase things on my behalf, e.g. travel bookings?

A great question! And one with layers.

If it's a rare occurrence then your VA can do the research on your gift or flights and then send you a link so you can make the purchase.

If it is more frequent then that may not be an ideal solution and you may want your VA to have access to a card.

The best way to organise this is to get for your VA, in their name, a credit or debit card. This can be from your bank or credit card provider, you can set up a physical credit card specifically for your VA. Call your bank if you need advice or how to set this up with them but make sure to tell them that your VA is not employed as that makes a difference.

Many business credit cards offer a system of virtual cards that you can issue as needed. These are limited so no one can spend thousands and then head off to Mauritius all expenses paid on your dime. You can switch virtual cards off at any time on an app as well as see how much has been spent. You can even issue them for a project, maybe flight booking, so you get the limit level right. This is ideal and for smaller, more agile businesses it's a great way to have your VA book flights, order gifts, reserve hotels etc. Because it's a named card and not shared, there is a clear way of tracking who spent what, when, if you are ever trying to track down receipts or figuring out what went wrong in the (hopefully very unlikely) event of things turning sour.

Occasionally, VAs might use their own cards for expenses and bill them back when they invoice. This might be what you agree between you for inexpensive items, but it's not appropriate for large amounts as they will be out of pocket until their invoice is paid.

What you should not do, is give your VA access to your own card so that they can use it on your behalf. You've almost certainly signed something somewhere with your bank that says you will not do that! Giving out your card details without checking with your bank that it's ok, will almost certainly lose you any protection that you have on fraudulent transaction.

Some VAs are given access to bank accounts and even make payments on behalf of their clients. One VA I spoke to even pays her own invoice along with all the others at month end! Everyone will have a different level of trust and you will get to a level that you feel comfortable with once your new VA has been with you a while.

If you are giving your VA access to your bank account and the permission to pay invoices etc, I'd suggest that you have in place a failsafe process for security. It's relatively easy for hackers to access emails or set up an email that looks like yours. It wouldn't be difficult for someone to send a scam email, pretending to be you, asking your VA to pay something. I'd suggest that any new suppliers or changes of bank account get a call to verify them based on a Google search for a number and that you personally approve any new suppliers with a call or a text to your VA in addition to an email.

Isn't it going to be a bit weird having someone in my inbox / calendar / life?

It certainly might feel strange at first having someone, and someone you barely know, in your work life, or possibly your home life. Remember that you always have control over how much your VA sees and, as you know, I would suggest a gentle start so that no one is thrown in the deep end.

But we VAs are very used to knowing a lot about those we support, and we are very discreet about what we see. In some inboxes we might be privy to conversations about team members or even board members, in others we might see medications that are ordered and whether you are a size 3 or a size 4 shoe. To be honest, the amount of information that I see a year I can now barely recall any of it and I certainly wouldn't disclose anything I saw to anyone else. The only caveat on that would be if I was aware of a client committing money laundering in which case I have to report them or I risk getting prosecuted. But have a workplace affair, a deep loathing of a co-worker or secret amateur dramatics hobby and our lips are sealed. Just remember that pretty much all the celebrities in the world have PAs who will have seen some awful things, I'm sure worse than anything we'd dig out of your inbox, and it is very rare that you hear about their PA spilling the beans.

My new VA is making a lot of mistakes

If this is a new VA, this might be a nasty case of the New Client Horrors.

When I first started as a VA I thought I was the only person to get the new client horrors, as I call them. But I'm not. I see it with my team and spend a fair amount of time mentoring VAs through this phase of work. It's important that you know about this bit of VA lore because it impacts on our early working relationship with you.

The New Client Horrors are a phenomenon where when you work with a new client you can't seem to do anything right. You start with delight and optimism as you get on your onboarding call with a new client. They download their brain to you along with multiple systems, all the info on their business and who's who and how to do this and that. And you panic. And you believe you can't do this. And then you make a tiny mistake, and you now KNOW you can't do this. And then because you are panic stricken and horrified about making another mistake right at the point when you should be your best self you are now a raving lunatic and so busy flapping you make another mistake and so begins a vicious circle of hell that can last anything from a couple of weeks to six months. I kid you not, I had this for six months with one client. We had a very long and very happy working relationship after this period, but the start was really tricky for me.

Not everyone gets it and not all clients seem to induce it. Honestly there doesn't seem to be a lot of logic behind it. However, when I dig into the New Client Horrors with a VA, particularly an experienced one, quite often there is something else on top of the new client that is going on in the background. I will never have one of my team start two new jobs close together, it's too much new information and too stressful. But if there is something going on in the VAs life, it's really easy for them to blame all the uncomfortable feelings on the new client when really the issue is life uncertainty AND a new client.

Examples where VAs have told me they aren't coping with a new client, or they can't do it, in the first week have turned out to be building an extension at home and living (and working) in a building site, moving house, having a bereavement in the family or ill health of a relative or problems with their marriage. When I think back to my six-month case, I had a nasty slipped disc and did my first call with that client lying on the floor trying not to sob in pain (camera off, obviously). And then a month later I had spinal surgery to fix said disc. Looking back, I very much doubt that she was the issue, I was. It was a really hard time balancing excruciating pain, strong drugs, client work and trying to live a life mostly from bed because anything other than lying down was not an option. It's unsurprising, as I look back, that I wasn't at my most robust emotionally!

I'm not saying you should give free reign to VAs messing up left right and centre, but in the early days, beware the new client horrors. If your VA is going through it, you need to tread carefully or you risk making it worse, which mean more mistakes, more panic and the whole thing can go south really fast. I would suggest scaling back what you give them to do, perhaps gently offer a refresher onboarding session or training if they feel they need it and be sure to notice and vocalise the tasks that have been successful.

My VA isn't quite working out and it's been long enough for them to settle in

Occasionally, even ignoring the new client horrors, things with a new VA don't seem to be settling into a routine or feeling quite right. Perhaps they are still making silly mistakes after what seems to be a reasonable time to have got to grips with the new role.

What are the mistakes they are making?

Is it that they aren't following instructions on a task, or aren't doing it the way you thought it should be done? If the latter, it might be that you need to be clearer about your expectations.

I recall one client telling me her VA had done a task badly. She had asked her to "go through my diary and pull out all the recurring meetings and all the team meetings so we can see when they are and make sure they are in a regular pattern". The VA sent her back a couple of paragraphs describing when the meetings were, who they were with and what the gaps were. But the client expected a spreadsheet. She hadn't asked for a spreadsheet but that was, in her mind, the best way to make sense of the information. VAs need clear instructions. Granted, the VA could and should have clarified how the client wanted the information presenting, but if she'd said up front, "can you go through my diary and add all recurring meetings and team meetings to a new spreadsheet so we can see them" that would have been a lot easier and saved some pain on both sides.

Could the mistakes have been lack of knowledge or lack of instruction, as in the example above? If so, try changing your communication or asking your VA to clarify their understanding of what you want before doing something if they aren't sure. It may just be that you aren't in a good communication rhythm yet.

If the mistakes are more user-error then that's different. Are you expecting your VA to do too much work in the time allotted? Going too fast can mean silly mistakes happen and if we're under pressure with a time budget we might not take the extra time to reread and check things. If that's the case you may need to rethink how much you can hand to your VA or how many hours are needed to accomplish your work.

VAs are human. We can and will mistakes just as everyone else does. Given the thousands of meetings I've put in over the course of my working life it's inevitable that I have ballsed some of those up. And I sure have. And flights. And probably lots else besides. No one is infallible. But there is a level of accuracy that you should expect from your VA.

I'd certainly make an allowance for a few silly mistakes in the first few weeks as they get to grips with you, your business and who's who. After that, I'd be starting to make a note of issues and having a conversation around accuracy. It's worth creating a list of their errors and evaluating whether it is a lack of knowledge about the company, a failure to understand a process or a genuinely silly and unnecessary mistake. Are they asking you questions or just consistently getting on with things and doing them wrong? Are they responding to your tasks to acknowledge they have got them and they are on them and then that they are done (in whatever form you've agreed that might take)? Silence is a concern. And it's best nipped in the bud early.

If they are aware that they are floundering but can't pull it back, then it's best to talk about it sooner than later. In that conversation, you can ask them what they need from you to help them. It may be nothing, it maybe they want a run through of something one more time as they haven't quite got to grips with it or it may be that they need just a bit more detail on tasks from you. But if you don't ask, you won't know.

How many mistakes is too many? Everyone has their tolerance levels and some mistakes are more impactful than others. Calling a valued client Dave instead of David in an email is one thing, sending every single email with at least one typo is quite another. If mistakes are making you nervous to trust your VA with anything other than basic tasks, this will become an issue.

If your VA has come through an agency, now would be the time to talk to the Lead VA. They might have some suggestions, or they can facilitate a discussion with the associate VA and see what might be going on for them.

Once you get to the point where you are worried about giving your VA any work, it's probably as well to cut your losses and move on. It can be hard to bounce back from a series of mistakes and rebuild that trust. As a freelance option, letting your VA go is pretty simple. You give them the notice that their contract requires. With any luck, one of the other shortlisted VAs still has some capacity or if there is an agency involved you can speak to the Lead VA and ask to switch resource.

If a VA makes a mistake, generally I'd expect them to

- Tell you at the first opportunity (not try and bluff it!)
- Apologise (to you and others as needed)
- Fix the problem ASAP
- Not repeat the same mistake twice

I wouldn't expect them to be charging time to fix their mistake. For really big mistakes where it costs you money, it may be that they should offer to make a financial contribution. In the (hopefully) very unlikely event of a really expensive mistake, this is why they have insurance.

My VA is great! How can I support them / thank them?

Everyone loves some appreciation and there are many ways you can thank your VA.

- Email them, tell them they are amazing. Do it often. It will make their day. It doesn't need to be an essay. "Thanks, you rock" works splendidly.
- Write them a more formal testimonial that they can use on their website or give them a LinkedIn recommendation.
- Offer to refer them to others (if they have capacity and you know someone), or perhaps your business can help them in other ways? I've been lucky enough to have clients join me on webinars, refer me to their connections or send great VAs to me that might be good for my team.
- Send them a gift or flowers or (my favourite) a handwritten card of thanks.
- Repeat the above as needed! It's really easy for a VA to become part of the furniture and somewhat overlooked, so we truly appreciate your recognition.

Conclusion

I very much hope that this book has answered any questions that you might have had about working with a Virtual Assistant. I also really hope that you have a clear understanding of the powerful positive impact that a good VA can have on you and your business—and exactly how to find the best VA for you and develop a wonderful working partnership.

We've looked at the things in your work that only you can do - your brilliance. This brilliance needs protecting so that you can do as much of it as you want to. That means that you need to make time and space. Time to spend on doing the things that are most valuable for you. And mental space to do it, without interruptions and the mental load of every single task in your role.

You also need to manage your energy so that when you launch into doing your brilliance, you have the mental capacity to be at your very best.

In many cases, your brilliance is what you sell. So being able to do more of it once you hire a VA directly impacts your profitability.

We also looked at work that you do that isn't your brilliance, but that possibly falls to you anyway, particularly in a small business where you have to wear many different hats during the course of the day. And ahead of any outsourcing we considered whether it might be possible to delete or automate anything.

We reflected on whether now is the right time to bring someone in, as well as on whether a VA is the right choice for you or if you should be looking for something else. Do you have enough work to make a decent VA role or is it a little too soon? Are there big life or work events coming up that might dictate when you should plan to hire and onboard someone so that you have enough bandwidth to give it plenty of time in the early stages?

We covered building and maintaining a great working relationship with your VA as well as how to get started in the best possible way by building your own "Bible of You" so that you know what exactly you do every day and how you do it. This can even be maintained by your VA so that there's an ongoing record of how processes work, who does what, and where information can be found.

As well as tasks, we considered what kind of values and personality might be a good fit for you in an assistant. What are the unwritten rules that you work by that might form part of your backpack – not contractual elements, but expectations that you have that you should be aware of?

When we looked at hiring a VA, we considered what you might need to include in a job description, how to go about the search, and how to sift through applicants and take meetings. I also shared the absolutely key things that I think are vital for any professional VA business to have to keep you and themselves safe. (You can read more about this in Annabel Kaye's Bonus Chapter coming up.)

We then covered the day-to-day aspects of working with a VA. How communication is vital to making this work and getting into a rhythm of task management and regular check ins to make sure everything is running smoothly.

Working with an amazing VA can help you hand over the tasks you shouldn't be doing. In addition, your VA can help you make your business more efficient and be a "second brain" to help you reduce your mental load. If you choose the right assistant, you can also expect some moral support, some cheerleading and even some fun as you get to know each other.

If you take nothing else away from this book, here are my top tips:

- Be clear that it is a VA that you need and not a PA or a different freelance expert.
- You must be happy to share them, to only work remotely unless agreed otherwise upfront, and to have minimal control of when and how they do your work. You also need to be OK with them potentially sending you a substitute.

- Delegate thoroughly and thoughtfully and take the time upfront to make the relationship work.
- Communicate well and often with your VA to keep the wheels moving.
- Respect their boundaries, pay them on time, and otherwise be a good client.
- Don't be nervous about having more than one VA, it's often a brilliant solution and won't cost you any more money. No one VA is amazing at everything or has unlimited capacity.
- Be willing to accept new ideas and feedback from your VA. They have years of experience and may well have some fabulous suggestions on how to make things run more smoothly.
- Review your VA relationship regularly. Don't miss chances to review and feedback on the service you are getting; it helps everyone get better.

Most of all, embrace it!

We live in amazing times when someone you have never met, that you may never meet in person, can be the glue that holds your business together. You have everything to gain by giving it a shot.

I wish you all the very best in your VA partnership. I'm excited for you at this new stage in your business!

Bonus Chapter: Keeping your Business Safe –
Some vital information from Annabel Kaye

It takes a lot of trust to hand things over to a VA. And there is some due diligence to do first to make sure that you, your clients, your data, and your Intellectual Property (IP) are protected in case anything goes wrong.

When it comes to things legal and financial, it's well worth paying for an expert to make sure you're keeping yourself safe. This Bonus Chapter covers some foundational areas to make you aware of them, but you will need to research further to see how legislation affects your business, as we're all different. Also, laws change. There will be up to date information out there if you look for it.

First, make sure your VA has the basics of a safe business set up. We covered this in the section on hiring. This means at least that they're taking being a VA seriously, it's not a way of making some extra cash and then they'll vanish into a puff of smoke once the big holiday or Christmas is paid for.

Second, whilst taking on a VA (or another freelancer) is pretty easy, contractually, there are more complicated pieces to be aware of on the data front and with employment law. I'm most definitely not an expert on either of these things. I did once bore the pants off some poor client at a networking event about IR35 and I can only apologise profusely and blame the free punch. I think in a futile effort to move away from the topic of law, I then moved onto decorating and gloss paint. Rich, I am sorry, there is no excuse for me. Sometimes I should not be let out in real life.

Fortunately, we have on hand a lady who is *actually* fun at parties—and who knows her stuff on all things legal for freelancers: legal expert, Annabel Kaye. Annabel and her team set up KoffeeKlatch in 2007 to provide freelancers with legal support, contracts and advice. In addition to running KoffeeKlatch, she now speaks regularly on her areas of expertise. Annabel knows her oats on employment law, IR35 and how that impacts freelancers, and the data protection laws that all businesses, including freelancers, need to work to in their businesses.

I want you to have the benefit of her expertise.

I therefore bribed her with a large gin, plonked one of her dogs on her lap, and sat down to pick her brains. Our conversation covered the areas that you absolutely don't want to fall foul of when you're bringing a VA into your business, as well as burning questions about all things legal. The results are here for you.

Annabel's details are in the Resources section if you want to reach out and get more advice based on your specific situation. She'll also suggest some websites (correct at the time of printing) for you to get further information on all the things we touch on. She has some great free videos you can watch too, to dig deeper into these topics. You can find all these links in the Resources section.

Annabel, let's start on IR35. What is it, how do I figure out if I need to worry about it, and what can happen if I mess it up?

That's a big subject, it could occupy the whole book.

IR35 has been around since the 2000's and is aimed at closing a tax loophole in which some contractors are actually working as employees in disguise. The terms of any contract will dictate whether a particular self-employed project is inside or outside of IR35 and there's an online form to check, project by project. If the contract is deemed to be inside IR35 then the client (employer) must deduct tax and National Insurance from the fees paid to the worker. Getting it wrong could cost you not only the unpaid tax, but also a financial penalty.

However, IR35 does not apply (at the moment) to all projects.

In a nutshell, if your VA has a limited company and you are above the threshold for making the assessments (currently an annual turnover of £10.2 million or more, having more than £5.1 million in the bank and no more than 50 employees) then you have to determine before you hire them whether your VA is "inside" or "outside" the scope of IR35. It's a completely stupid idea. I'll be quoted on that because even HMRC get their own assessments wrong and they're the people in charge of it.

So our brilliant government's idea is that you should actually be more accurate in making this determination than they are. But only if you're above the threshold. So for the vast majority of people hiring VAs, there are only two things you need to know:

- *One, does your VA have a limited company?*
- *And two, are you above the threshold?*

If the answer to the first one is "no" and the answer to the second one's "no" then you don't need to worry in terms of IR35. If you do hit both those criteria, it's worth checking out the gov.uk "Check employment status for tax" assessment online.

If you don't hit the criteria for IR35, you do still need to look at the Pay as You Earn (PAYE) regulations instead. You need to make sure that you are hitting the criteria HMRC lay out that means someone is a contractor, not a "worker".

If your VA does not have a limited company, then it's always your responsibility, not theirs, to consider whether they should be on PAYE instead of being a contractor. If you're treating your VA like an employee but just calling them 'self-employed', that will fail the test.

There are a number of tests to determine whether a person working for you is a "worker" or a contractor. Do see the Resources section for a free course you can do to find out more as well as an online form from HMRC where you can check your VA's relationship with you against all the criteria.

What exactly is a "worker" under the law? What are the differences between that and being employed or self-employed?

The ultimate distinctions are about control and about whether the person can send a substitute.

When you work as an employee you'll be told "this is the software we use, this is where you work, this is when you work" and so on. That's how it works when you have a job, isn't it? If you didn't want to work next week and you had a job and you said to your boss, "I'm sending my sister, she's

really good at what I do", they'll say, "you must be joking".
You plainly have a job, don't you?

If on the other hand you're providing your own equipment
(you'll obviously be accessing your client's own software
because of GDPR), and you could send a substitute if you
were sick or wanted to, you are self-employed. You're running
your own business.

The problem is there are three categories, not two.

There are people who have a job, as we've just described. There
are people running a business, as we've just described. And,
unhelpfully, in the middle there are "workers". Workers are
people who do everything the same as self-employed people
except they aren't able to send a substitute. So, if you say to
your VA "it's always got to be you", they are workers. (Unless
they're trading through a limited company, in which case we
go back to IR35 and the criteria that apply there.)

If they're a worker, you don't owe them unfair dismissal
rights, as they're not a fully-fledged employee. But you do owe
them, among many other things, statutory holiday pay and a

full set of equality rights, which are the ones most people are scared of.

So, if you hire a VA you need to move on from the never-ending paranoia of "I don't want my VA to substitute". It's not only putting you at risk of your VA costing you more money than you thought by incurring all these worker rights and costs, but if you make them an employee by accident, unlike IR35, there are no thresholds. Whatever size business you are, it applies and it's your job to assess whether they should be on Pay as You Earn.

If you treat someone to all intents and purposes like an employee, but just pay them as a non-employee, HMRC can come back to you for all the Pay as You Earn you should have paid, with penalties. Which is a 50% uplift with interest. And they can demand it in 14 days. So if you're sitting there thinking "I could never let my VA send a substitute to my business", you really need an employee. Don't even go down the self-employed route.

Is it about how much control you want?

Exactly. Because if you need to be in total control, hire someone as an employee. You can hire someone on a zero hours contract, you can hire a flexi hours person, you can hire all sorts of things – it doesn't have to be a 40 hours a week employee, but don't muck about in this area because it could come back to bite you.

Now people say, "I've never heard of it coming back to bite you". Well, sure. The thing is you never do—because when HMRC come for them, people settle up quietly if they've got the money. Do you think they're all over Facebook going, "I just got dinged for five grand"? You'll never hear about it. Their accountants will bury it and they'll take the hit.

It doesn't happen a lot. But it does happen. We hear of about four or five a year for my entire client base. That might be a very small percentage, but the trouble is if it's you, it's a 100% happening to you. It's not a little bit happening to you. It's all academic until it's you.

What should a contract for a self-employed person cover and why? And do I really need a contract for a little bit of work?

Yes. You need a contract.

Generally, I'd expect a service provider to offer me a contract. I use my own because I have nine VAs, and having them all on their own different contracts would do my head in. It doesn't really matter whose it is as long as you have one. There are a number of reasons why you should.

One is about data. If your VA is even viewing personal data about your prospects, your team or your suppliers, it's not lawful for them to touch it without a written data processing agreement. So, as far as that goes, the days of doing business on a handshake are gone. Any reasonable VA wouldn't do it. And those that are telling you they are willing to are telling you that they're inexperienced as VAs. That means that if you choose to work with them, you need to be extra, doubly careful about specifying how your data is handled.

In our VA contracts, we include a data processing agreement because we find it confusing having multiple agreements. So we do it all in one.

Whether it's together with a main contract or separate, it's a legal requirement that you have some signed form that covers the fundamental basics of a DPA (Data Processing Agreement):

- *Who's got access to the information and for what purpose?*
- *For how long do they have it?*
- *To do what with it?*
- *Specify that data is kept confidential.*
- *Specify what the security infrastructures are to make that happen.*

This DPA ends your legal obligation! You're not in the least bit legally required to protect your business with any other contract. You are perfectly entitled to wander about blind and make a mess of things if you want!

But it would be a jolly good idea to have a good contract that expresses the VA to be self-employed. And you have to treat them as if they are, because the contract won't protect you if it's stuff and nonsense. So, it's no good managing them like an employee and contracting them as self-employed. You have to do the things in the contract that tick those boxes.

Unlike an employee, anything an independent contractor or a freelancer creates for you, the copyright belongs to them. A contract is a common mechanism of transferring stuff they write uniquely for you to you – either as a copyright or as a licence. So, if you are building a brand or content that you want to be able to use and reuse long after you and the VA part ways, you really do need to sort that out in the contract.

You probably also want a "confidentiality agreement". The Americans call them an "NDA", and this has drifted into British parlance. These help you make sure your VA understands what they can and cannot share outside of your team. Any responsible VA wouldn't be sharing anything anyway. But sometimes it's not clear what's confidential information and what's stuff that everyone should know. A good confidentiality agreement would allow you to define that in a way that's clear to both of you. What's not helpful is to have 38 pages of legal jargon that neither of you understand because then you can't quite be sure who's agreed to what.

So, data protection, copyright transfer, and confidentiality are the absolute fundamentals for the contract. In terms of protecting your business and the VA, I think it's also a really good idea to be clear in the contract about:

- *Exactly what you're paying them to do*
- *How often and how frequently, and how much of it*

At KoffeeKlatch, the biggest arguments we see between VAs and clients (and we support both) are around the client wanting more and more and the VA thinking "I'm not being paid for this", but the client thinking they've already paid. So, it's best to have up-front, absolute clarity about what's included in any retainers, project prices, fixed fees, however you do it, and what's not included. And even if you're looking at an hourly rate agreement, be realistic about what can be done in an hour or two hours. It's no good hiring a VA for two hours a month and then wanting 20 hours' work. And vice versa, by the way—don't retain a VA for 40 hours a month and send them one email to write. Be sensible.

And that often means having an initial trial period to work it out. Not everyone knows in advance how long things might take. Contract that trial period.

And as to the small piece of work question, if the small piece of work involves handling personal data, read my lips, you always need the data protection agreement. If the small piece of work involves copyright and you want to own it, you always need to contract it. I recommend trying to get everyone contracted from the off because when does the small piece of work become big enough to justify a contract? It's better business hygiene to say "everyone we pay is on a contract" just as we pay everyone by BACS, or Wise or PayPal. Have a system and just follow it.

It is hard when you get your first VA because you think, "I don't like admin, so I'm getting a VA to do admin, and now I've got to do admin to get the VA."

But your VA should have a contract that should sort you out. And if your VA doesn't and they haven't even bothered to attempt to set one up, they're telling you they are very, very new in the business. And that tells me you need to check what platforms they're on, whether they're sharing their laptop, whether they're using free software. Because often that's a big data security problem. It tells me they're not good to go.

And now, everyone's favourite. Data. We touched on it as we talked about contracts. What should we be thinking about in terms of data protection for our businesses when we are bringing in outside support? What even is data in a business?

I don't like the word data because I've never once woken up and thought, "I need to do data collection today." Just think of it as information—it's easier. Do you have information about people in your business?

Now data is not just names and addresses and email addresses, all of which are information about people. It's not just single bits alone. It also covers information about people that if you put it together, would allow you to identify an individual. So, for example, you might have an email address that goes to info@, but if you've also got a mobile number of the person who answers that email and you know who that person is, when you combine the mobile number and info@ email address, that person is identified. So, it's not just information about a person, it's pieces of information that you can put together to identify someone. Even if you haven't ever bothered to do it.

For that reason, almost everyone in business handles personal data. Imagine a way of working where you didn't have client names on your phone, so when they ring up you have no idea who's calling? That's personal data. What name belongs to that phone number? Because not all those numbers are corporate numbers, are they? They're personal mobiles. Even corporate emails that identify people by name can be personal data. So obviously, if the email is john@jiflips.com, there might be 10 Johns. But the minute you put a surname in, the chances are there's only one John with that surname and that's personal data. So, it's a nonsense to think you don't collect personal data even if you don't have a database and you only work business to business.

The next big nonsense we hear is, "well my VA doesn't process data, she just views my diary or views whatever".

I have news for you: viewing information is processing it. Picking it up, looking at it, changing nothing and putting it down is processing it. There's direct European case law to that effect. And the reason for that is viewing it puts little things in your cache that are downloaded to your laptop or your phone. That's processing it, and you can't view it without that going on. Not unless you're in a high-tech global surveillance business and you know how to do that.

Some people are so scared of complying with it they spend more time and energy on not complying than they would ever have spent on complying with the regulations. It's a bit like tax really. Some people spend £20,000 on accountants to avoid paying £2,000 worth of tax. Where's the sense in that? Just be reasonable. Everyone collects data and that means that you've got to be sensible about not collecting too much. Don't be greedy, don't keep information everywhere just in case. You've got to keep it for a reason and there are only six reasons. If you can't tick one of those boxes, you can't keep it and you can't steal it from other places and use it.

If your mate's car was bought for their business - say they've got a window cleaning business and you're a hairdresser and you decide to steal their car and use it for your business, that's theft, right? Think of data like the car. It's not your data, so don't do it. People are very greedy. They think "oh just a little bit. It doesn't matter. It doesn't count" but it does count because if you start emailing people that have never heard of you, you quite often get your emails sent into spam and blocked. And then your email deliverer starts going, "I'm not carrying your traffic because you're a rubbish sender". It has consequences. But the problem is the consequences are later than the event so you can't join up the dots.

You need to secure data. When it comes to having a VA, you should let your VA enter your own systems and avoid arrangements where the VA holds data within their systems that you can't get your hands on. Because it's your job to turn the VA off when the contract ends, not the VA's to turn you off. You're supposed to be the Data Controller and control means having access.

If you don't know what you're doing, you need to get someone who knows data to sort you out, not say "it can't apply to me because I don't understand it".

Obviously, we've now been through Brexit. I have heard folks say that we don't need to worry about the General Data Protection Regulations (GDPR) anymore. Does it still count?

Yes, it still counts. There are more than 137 countries in the world—and more every day—that have a form of data privacy.

Europe led the way, but it hasn't stood still while we've been busy working through Brexit. It is highly unlikely that the UK is going to have no form of data privacy legislation, whether the words GDPR fade from what we call it or not. We've got a data privacy bill going through parliament as we speak, and it's not repealing GDPR, it's just rebranding it into UK language. And there are some minor tricks and tweaks. But the only countries in the world that don't have laws like this are Russia, Somalia, and Ethiopia and I'm sincerely hoping that we're not going to be joining that club. Even America, which doesn't have federal-level laws, has state-level laws about data privacy.

So, the idea that post-Brexit data protections don't apply to us is a bit cuckoo. And by the way, quite a lot of the trade many companies do is with other countries. There are also quite a lot of cross-border VAs who are in the UK with clients in Canada, America etc. As well as clients in the UK who are hiring VAs from overseas. Their whole team may not be in the same country. We do have to observe the relevant data privacy laws and it is a bit trickier cross border.

One of the sections in this book looks at ways to check that your VA is properly set up to run a business. I'd say ICO registration, insurance and having a contract are the most essential. Is there anything else you would add to that list?

Do they have their own data privacy policy? Because even though that wouldn't apply to the data you are sharing with them, it applies to your data as an individual doing business with them. And if they haven't got far enough down the road to realise they need a policy and processes, it's not a good indicator of how they would understand handling the data you share with them.

One other thing I've got on that list is professional versions of software. Not home versions or student versions or a mate's version.

Absolutely. And it's tied to device sharing, which is one of the big issues in data security, particularly for VAs not in the UK.

In developing countries, devices that we buy on a month's salary cost two years' salary. So, it's quite common for people to device share. And you get it here in the UK with the bottom end of the market - their kids use their laptop when they're not working. This can be a massive security risk and we put draft security rules into our contracts so you mustn't do it. But where we're aware of a reason where it has to be done, we always make sure the VA has an admin account set up that they don't use day to day—so that anything that's phished doesn't spread. Unfortunately, quite often if they've got student, personal or free software, they can't add that admin account. It's one of the many reasons why I recommend avoiding cheap-as-chips, side-hustle VAs. The price of having a separate device, or at least professional software, is part of what's included in a VA's appropriate market rate.

When my mechanic wants to use £10,000 worth of equipment on my car and charge me £200 for a service, do I say, "Well I'll take it to a mate. I want to pay less. I'd much prefer to guess if my car's safe"? No, I pay for someone who has invested in proper equipment to keep me safe. Same story for the VAs.

We all think that everything is covered in the contract, but really everyone has their own invisible list of things that they think should happen. I've talked about understanding and sharing those invisible expectations as unpacking your backpack. What's in your backpack?

The biggest item in my backpack is that I'm looking for someone to solve problems. That means that when I'm having that initial call with them, I'm always trying to find out what problems they solved to get to that point. Because if the answer's none, you know, that means they just ponied up and copied everyone else's stuff, got a few downloads and thought "well I'll be a VA". They may be at the beginning of their journey, and I might use them for some very, very, very low-level work as a one off. I'll give them a couple of hours of work. But I wouldn't go further than that because a big part of my backpack, and I suspect a lot of business owners, is I hire VAs to make my life easier, not more difficult.

In fact, most of my backpack is about what is now called mindset, which is not a phrase in its modern manifestation that I'm very happy with. I prefer the word attitude. They don't have to agree with me politically, emotionally, diet wise. You know, I love dogs, they can love cats. It's not an issue.

But can they solve problems? Will they go and find out something and come back with a suggestion or will they wait for me to feed them? I will certainly have to feed them logins. And access. But once that's done, I need a mind in the virtual room.

The other expectation that I've learned to decode is about priorities. There's a subset of VA who will vanish and say, "I just couldn't be doing that because my family comes first". My family's always come first too, and I've never once said that to a client. It's not necessary to say that, and if they do it's a red flag to me of a side-hustle VA. Talk to them about why they're a VA because if you are trying to build an ambitious business and you need support and they're a side-hustle VA this is going to come unstuck pretty quickly. And don't expect to pay side-hustle rates for a career VA who's running a serious team of professionals.

To a degree you get what you pay for. So, if your backpack is, you know, "I'm after ultimately getting where an executive PA would get me internally" your side-hustle type VA is the junior typist. Are you sure about this decision? They're not going to solve your problems. They're not going to build your business with you. They're not going to be a big part of the team. They're just going to be a task monkey.

And that's fine if a task monkey is what you want. But then don't get cross with them when you ask them to do something, and they can't. One of my favourites is when nothing ever comes back from a VA and then you chase them down and you ask, "what happened"? And they say, "I didn't know how to do it". And they haven't even got the initiative to get back to you and say, "I'm stuck".

So, there's a wide range, from people who can run your company for you to people who can't figure out whether they can or cannot do something. And generally speaking, they charge different rates. I'm not saying everyone that charges a lot is brilliant and everyone who doesn't charge a lot is rubbish, but it takes time and experience and equipment to put that skillset set together. And trying to buy it cheap can be a mistake.

All of these expectations mean I don't resist thorough onboarding the way a lot of new VA hirers do. Onboarding's difficult because it has to be done correctly to achieve my objectives. But I'd rather spend six hours onboarding a VA that stayed with me two years than spend 20 minutes and have another one next month and another one next month and another one next month. I don't understand shortcutting that.

One thing that I'm really clear on in this book is that getting a VA doesn't relieve you of responsibility. You still have to understand how your own business works.

Oh, absolutely. You can delegate the work, but you can never delegate the responsibility. You are the person who goes to jail if this goes tits up. You are the person who gets sued if this goes tits up. Now I don't want to be paranoid, but you can't say "well I gave some VA the keys to my business three years ago and I've never seen her since. But I thought she was doing a good job". It's not a defence in law to anything. And although we don't build businesses to defend ourselves from being sued, we build businesses to give ourselves the life we want, you still have to have that in mind.

Finally, you have a good set of VAs yourself. What top tips would you give anyone taking on a VA for the first time?

Well, my top tip, and I'm sure it's been covered elsewhere, is not to think of yourself as ultimately having one VA who does everything. If you need a fabulous diary manager, odds are they're probably not going to be good at sorting out web design updates or graphic design. They might be, but being brilliant at everything is a gift not given to all of us! And I think you need to look very hard at what you want done in the foreseeable future and get, for now, someone who's good at that.

I tend to start people with limited tasks, but not limited contracts so that I can build out from success without re-contracting them. And I always give them the lowest possible access to stuff until I'm fairly confident of their working methods. Obviously, I'd never give people admin rights to any technology when they are new on my team. I don't believe in just handing people my logins and walking away. I'd be giving them the keys to my business, my income, my house and my life. I'm very controlling about some elements of onboarding people, but then I do give them a task and let them get on with it because I need to see how they do that without me on the phone every day chasing them. And if I never hear from them again, which has happened, I'll just switch them off at the end of month.

Wow. That's a concern. They just vanished?

Yes, because they lack the get up and go to get up and go.

It isn't many. I've had about one a year.

How many VAs do you have at the moment?

It's about nine. They're all very specialised. But the other thing I've done is each VA's got a specialism and what I would call a second rank specialism that covers another VA's first rank specialism. I think they used to call that manpower planning. So that if one VA goes under a bus, we've got someone who knows how we work generally who can sub that. It's always bothered me the idea of having my entire business in the hands of one self-employed person somewhere else.

Particularly if I would then be mad enough not to let them send a substitute.

Thank you so much for your time, Annabel, and for the insightful and non-jargony look at the legal side of working with a VA.

I hope that Annabel's no-nonsense look at the legal side of outsourcing has given you some food for thought.

To summarise the key points:

- Make sure you aren't treating your self-employed VA as a "worker." In particular, be happy for them to send a substitute to cover their work. Use the HRMC website to check (see Resources).
- Ensure you and they both understand what they're doing with your data – you must have some form of data processing agreement for all VA work.
- A contract and NDA, or confidentiality agreement, is not essential but highly recommended.
- As another business, a VA owns the copyright to any work they do unless you have a contract that says otherwise. Many contracts might say that the VA owns the copyright until the work is paid for as a failsafe against non-payment.

- You get what you pay for – a properly set up VA or VA agency will cost more because they are paying for the right equipment, licences and knowledge to keep themselves and you safe.

There are links to more information at the end of the book in the Resources section.

Acknowledgements

Since writing my last book I'd honestly forgotten how flipping hard it is! Particularly alongside a very busy day job.

Thanks to my amazing Ops VA Helen for the encouragement and support, including those WhatsApp messages saying "Why are you in your inbox? Write stuff!" which made me chuckle.

To the wider Personally Virtual team—thanks for showing me how utterly brilliant VAs can be. You all amaze me every day with your dedication, skills and attitude. Particular thanks go to Vicki Doudelle and Claire Ennion for leading the charge in busy teams while I've been knee deep in editing rounds.

Thanks to all the VAs who completed my survey on their experiences of working with clients and those that shared it in their networks.

To those who let me interview them, formally or informally, about their experiences working with a VA or VAs, I am deeply grateful.

Thanks to the SVA (Society of Virtual Assistants) and APVA (Association of Professional Virtual Assistants) for their efforts in creating surveys to give us great data on the UK VA industry. It is a huge amount of work which is often unappreciated.

To my brother and sister-in law who generously let me use their holiday home to write the first draft, thank you. What a stunning location to write in.

In no particular order, grateful thanks for contributions and moral support go to Richard Williams, Claire Stibbon and Laura Green.

Thanks to Annabel Kaye for completing an interview about topics that I really wanted readers to have some more detailed knowledge on.

And lastly, to my dogs, now older and wiser than when I wrote the first book. Thank you for not destroying anything in the house while I was head down on my laptop, it's appreciated.

About the Author

Kathy Soulsby has run her Virtual Assistant business, Personally Virtual, since 2014.

Personally Virtual now comprises a team of over 30 VAs, supporting businesses great and small with expert diary ninja and operational support. As the business has grown, her role has focused less on doing the work and more on finding and recruiting amazing VAs, matching them up with the right clients, and monitoring their relationships as they grow.

One of her proudest moments was receiving an email from a client simply saying, "Thank you for matching me with XXXX, she's f***ing brilliant". Kathy has had many longer and less sweary testimonials from clients, as well as from happy VAs that adore their Personally Virtual client, but this one appealed greatly for its brevity and heartfelt wording!

Prior to setting up Personally Virtual, Kathy was an EA for 16 years. Before accidentally embracing the world of business support, Kathy's career after graduation spanned restaurant and pub management, recruitment, customer complaints and shellfish sales.

A passionate advocate of the PA, EA and VA industry, Kathy believes that being an EA or VA is a fantastic career choice and that a good assistant can be life changing for those getting the support.

She is a total productivity nerd, and she loves nothing more than a new way to get things done more efficiently, whether that's a book, a task system or a methodology.

Outside of running a business and writing, Kathy can often be found in a field with her two collies doing agility or flyball or dunking herself into unnecessarily cold water for a wild swim.

Resources

Legal

- *Annabel Kaye:* IR35 and GDPR expert: https://www.koffeeklatch.co.uk/

Data Protection

- https://www.gov.uk/data-protection

Employment Law / IR35

- https://www.koffeeklatch.co.uk/store/product/ir35-mini-course (code FreeIR35)
- https://www.gov.uk/guidance/check-employment-status-for-tax
- https://www.gov.uk/guidance/understanding-off-payroll-working-ir35

ADHD

- ADHD Access to Work application form: https://www.get-disability-work-support.service.gov.uk/apply/
- Flown Co-working and body doubling sessions https://flown.com/

Other Resources

- Personally Virtual – www.personallyvirtual.co.uk
- Kathy's first book: Virtually Painless, The Unedited Reality of Moving from Personal Assistant to Virtual Assistant, PA to VA, Employee to Business Owner https://www.personallyvirtual.co.uk/books/
- Kim Arnold, email writing expert: https://www.kimarnold.co.uk/

Tech Resources

- Typeform to use to create an application form (or if you already use Microsoft 365 try MS Forms, if you're a Google Suite person, try Google Forms as they do the same thing)

- Doodle Poll – a website that helps you find times that work for multiple people.
- Quick Steps. An Outlook tool (currently not available on Outlook for Mac, sorry!) that combines multiple steps like forwarding, categorising and filing for speedier email management.
- Boomerang. Available in Gmail and Outlook to "bring back" messages on the date you request or delay sending of an email (so you can prepare a series of emails in advance, perhaps confirming a series of events).
- Calendly, Acuity Scheduling and more – online sites that allow you to set up links so people can book directly into your diary.

Further reading

- Dan Sullivan, Doctor Benjamin Hardy, et al., Who Not How: The Formula to Achieve Bigger Goals Through Accelerating Teamwork
- Cal Newport, Deep Work: Rules for Focused Success in a Distracted World
- Daniel H. Pink, When: The Scientific Secrets of Perfect Timing

- Jan Jones, The CEO's Secret Weapon: How Great Leaders and Their Assistants Maximize Productivity and Effectiveness
- Michael Hyatt, The Virtual Assistant Solution: come up for Air, Offload the Work you Hate, and Focus on What you do Best
- Chris Ducker, Virtual Freedom: How to work with Virtual Staff to Buy More Time, Become More Productive and Build Your Dream Business
- Jess Ostroff, Panic Proof: How the Right Virtual Assistant Can Save Your Sanity and Grow Your Business
- Alex Soojung-Kim Pang, Rest; Why you get More Done When You Work Less
- Paul Aldrich and Andrew Pullman, Building an Outstanding Workforce
- David Mellor, From Crew to Captain: Commander of the Fleet
- Adam Hergenrother, Hallie Warner et al, The Founder and the Force Multiplier

Appendix – Task Management Apps

A task management app can be a huge help when you are collaborating with a VA. It gives you somewhere to brain dump things that need doing for your VA and your VA has somewhere to track tasks and ask you for more information if needed.

In this section I'm just going to lightly skim over some of my favourite apps. There are thousands out there and your VA may very well already use one which they are happy to recommend.

Simple task apps

Todoist

This is a really simple app. It works online or on a Mac, phone or PC. It's a list. It's a very pretty and fairly customisable list. The free version is really good, and you can add as many people as you need to without extra cost. You can have multiple projects, so things are easy to find and there are tags and comments to keep on top of things. You can turn an email into a task by emailing it to Todoist, which I find very handy. It's a great starter.

Microsoft To Do

This used to be Tasks back in the day but has had a pretty major upgrade—now it's a sexy list, rather than a really ugly list tucked away behind your emails. If you already pay for a Microsoft 365 subscription, you'll get To Do included in that so it's worth a look. If you use Outlook and Teams, then it integrates pretty nicely to save you retyping stuff. Flagged emails appear in your list as well (this may or may not be extremely irritating for you, you decide) and you get all the context from emails as they are attached. If you're already paying money and you don't need anything too fancy, this could be the one for you.

Trello

Trello is sexy boxes rather than a sexy list—a Kanban, in fact—and those with a more visual or tactile way of working generally love it. Trello is made up of boards and on each board are cards (a bit like post-it notes). You can add a picture to a card as well as checklists and notes. So, you might use one board as a contacts board and add a photo or a company logo. As a task list, the usual way it works is to have each card as a task and have the cards moving left to right from a column of "new" or "not started" across "in progress" or "waiting for reply" until landing in the far right "done" column. Within each card you can have subtasks, notes, all sorts. And you can have tags. It's quite popular and suits some people, others find it a bit messy to find all that they need to do.

Business management and project apps

If you want more than just a pretty-looking list, you need to consider a more complex system. These are getting better and more user-friendly all the time. With some of these more complex ones, getting an expert (VA?) on the set-up can be really helpful. In large part because they can do so much, you can get a lot more out of it than you think is possible if you get an expert to set it up for you.

These are perhaps suited more to bigger teams, but I used ClickUp for years before anyone collaborated with me on it, it just keeps things moving swiftly and means I don't forget things. We looked earlier at automation and this kind of system is precisely the kind of thing that can help you do that.

ClickUp

One app to rule them all, is their strapline. Possibly liberated from a fantasy film, but I could be wrong. I'm not that nerdy. ClickUp doesn't quite live up to its line — I still have other apps for Finance and for email — but it is certainly getting there. And I love it.

Aside from extremely sexy lists, you can view your data or your tasks in the form of a Kanban (like a Trello Board), a mind map (this book is in mind map form), calendar, table (like a spreadsheet) and many more. So you can cut the same data in many ways and anyone on the team can do the same, so if they prefer a list and you prefer a board, you are both happy. You can allocate tasks to others, add comments and keep a trail of conversation so a task can become a repository for documents and ideas as well as subtasks and checklists.

ClickUp is very customisable, so it can easily be used as a CRM system, a content planner and many other things. One of my favourite things about it is the ability to create forms. I can send a link to someone, who fills in a form and it appears as a task with all the information I need. I use this for new clients, for example, so I can get accurate information to create a contract. It's much quicker for the new client to fill in a quick form than to type everything out in an email. I also use it as an application form for jobs.

It also has automations, so you can set emails to go out, move tasks on a specific date, on their due date and any manner of other things you might dream up.

Monday

Monday, or "the posh ClickUp" as I tend to think of it, can really run some big businesses. It's very similar to ClickUp. It's more expensive and I don't think it's as user-friendly, but I've not spent as many millions of hours in it as I have in ClickUp. Data is easy to see and customise and there are add-ons you can purchase if you want some created sections, like HR or a CRM.

Printed in Great Britain
by Amazon